THE BARS

1 - **Achilles Heel** *180 West Street*
2 - **Ba'sik** *323 Graham Avenue*
3 - **Bushwick Country Club** *618 Grand Street*
4 - **Clover Club** *210 Smith Street*
5 - **Dear Bushwick** *41 Wilson Avenue*
6 - **Donna** *27 Broadway*
7 - **Dram** *177 S 4th Street*
8 - **The Drink** *228 Manhattan Avenue*
9 - **Extra Fancy** *302 Metropolitan Avenue*
10 - **Fort Defiance** *365 Van Brunt Street*
11 - **Grand Army** *336 State Street*
12 - **Grand Ferry Tavern** *229 Kent Avenue*
13 - **Hotel Delmano** *82 Berry Street*
14 - **Huckleberry Bar** *588 Grand Street*
15 - **Leyenda** *221 Smith Street*
16 - **Long Island Bar** *110 Atlantic Avenue*
17 - **Loosie Rouge** *91 South 6th Street*
18 - **Maison Premiere** *298 Bedford Avenue*
19 - **The Narrows** *1037 Flushing Avenue*
20 - **Pork Slope** *247 5th Avenue*
21 - **Quarter Bar** *676 5th Avenue*
22 - **The Richardson** *451 Graham Avenue*
23 - **Roberta's** *261 Moore Street*
24 - **The Shanty/New York Distilling Co.** *79 Richardson Street*
25 - **Tooker Alley** *793 Washington Avenue*

BROOKLYN BARTENDER

A MODERN GUIDE TO
COCKTAILS and SPIRITS

BROOKLYN BARTENDER

A MODERN GUIDE TO COCKTAILS *and* SPIRITS

CAREY JONES

photographs by LUCY SCHAEFFER

illustrations by REBECCA MATT

DEDICATION
To John McCarthy, and a lifetime of shaking and stirring together

Black Dog & Leventhal Publishers
Hachette Book Group
1290 Avenue of the Americas
New York, NY 10104

www.hachettebookgroup.com

www.blackdogandleventhal.com

Printed in China
Cover design by Ohioboy Design
Interior design by Red Herring Design

IM

First Edition: May 2016
10 9 8 7 6 5 4 3 2 1

Black Dog & Leventhal Publishers is an imprint of Hachette Books, a division of Hachette Book Group. The Black Dog & Leventhal Publishers name and logo are trademarks of Hachette Book Group, Inc.

The Hachette Speakers Bureau provides a wide range of authors for speaking events. To find out more, go to www.HachetteSpeakersBureau.com or call (866) 376-6591.

The publisher is not responsible for websites (or their content) that are not owned by the publisher.

Library of Congress Cataloging-in-Publication Data available upon request.

ISBN: 978-0-316-39025-5

Table Of
CONTENTS

THE NARROWS

French 75, Achilles Heel

INTRODUCTION

Rarely, if ever, has it been so easy to drink so well as in modern-day Brooklyn.

Really, the allure of "Brooklyn"—as a borough, and as a concept—has never been stronger. In the last decade, it's gained a reputation as a New York cultural hub in its own right, the less-buttoned-up borough, a place driven by youth and creativity. Whereas once it was assumed that everything interesting or relevant in New York happened in Manhattan, today, if anything, the opposite holds true. Manhattanites regularly cross the river for dinner and a night out—a notion that would have felt somewhat bizarre a decade ago.

And nowhere is Brooklyn's creativity, energy, and spirit more on display than in its bars. Defined by far more than their drinks, bars occupy a central space in the New York social world, each with its own character, its distinct quirks and rituals, its community of fans and regulars who, for whatever reason, respond to the energy of a space. "Bars are our community centers," says Del Pedro of Brooklyn's Tooker Alley. "Literally, in that they're secular places for people to commune—and how many of those are there in New York?"

And the rise of modern mixology coincides with Brooklyn's emergence as a cultural force. Today, mixologists are regarded with the same awe as chefs; there's a genuine respect for the artistry behind the bar. We are in the midst of a cocktail renaissance, perhaps the first golden age of the cocktail since Prohibition swept away much of America's drinking culture (and forced underground what it didn't).

Craft cocktails, in some ways, emerged as a reaction to the drinking culture of the 1980s and 1990s—where alcohol was often a status symbol (see: Grey Goose and Patrón) or purely utilitarian (see: Budweiser). But in more recent years, a cultural shift took hold. Craft brewing took off. Wine enthusiasts turned from high-dollar Chardonnays and Cabernets to lesser-known grapes and regions. Small, independent restaurants with highly original cuisine stole the focus from more traditional establishments.

And cocktails were no different. During many years of flavored vodka and four-liqueur shooters, classics were considered old-fashioned; with the major exception of the Martini, many classic cocktails just weren't on the radar. Nonetheless, some bartenders were inspired to look to the past—unearthing early vintage cocktail books and studying the sophisticated drinking culture of decades, and even centuries, back. And slowly, at restaurant bars and, eventually, dedicated cocktail bars, mixology gained traction.

As with any creative discipline, there's a balance between tradition and innovation. Studying the classics gave bartenders insight into cocktail structure, balance, and rigor, into time-tested ingredients, methods, and principles. But armed with that knowledge, it's natural for a creative impulse to take over. Today's cocktail world is simultaneously backward-looking, to that still-often-untapped canon of elegant, time-honored classics—and forward-looking, embracing the new spirits, liqueurs, and bitters on the market, pulling unexpected ingredients into the cocktail world.

Fast-forward to the mid-2000s, and cocktail bars were popping up all over Manhattan, led by such influential bars as Milk & Honey, Pegu Club, Flatiron Lounge, and Employees Only, with Death + Co. and PDT soon following. These bars not only established reputations in their own right, helping to make cocktails exciting and relevant again, they also trained up generations of bartenders in their house styles, and to house standards—and many of their acolytes went on to open bars of their own.

Cocktail culture made enormous strides in these years. Bartenders found a willing audience ready to appreciate their creations, from revived classics of the past to innovations of their own. And trailblazing cocktail bars were meticulous in their craft, fighting hard to differentiate themselves from their less sophisticated counterparts, constantly pushing boundaries. But many Manhattan bars developed an attitude and aesthetic that fellow bartenders grew tired of. The temples to "mixology": dark, clubby-feeling bars that took their craft so seriously there wasn't much room for fun, and the "speakeasy" aesthetic that felt more exclusive than subversive.

"One of the things I was disappointed in was how formal cocktail bars could be—and obnoxious and condescending and elitist," says Del Pedro, who spent decades behind the stick in Manhattan. "It was a lifestyle thing—we're *this* kind of bar that wants *this* kind of person. That always bothered me."

Meanwhile, Brooklyn continued to gain attention in the public eye, as Manhattan rents pushed more and more residents and, eventually, businesses out to Brooklyn. Many of the 20- and 30-something mixology enthusiasts who crowded Manhattan bars lived in Brooklyn—not to mention the bartenders and bar owners, who often did as well. Many now-beloved Brooklyn venues got their start when an owner saw a need in the neighborhood he or she lived in; if they couldn't find a proper cocktail close to home, why not open a bar that could deliver?

And while mixology did come to Brooklyn, the attitude didn't follow suit. While accepting all the advancements in the cocktail world, many barfolk crossing the bridge sought to create a different kind of establishment—with the comfort and camaraderie and, frankly, fun of a less formal bar, but with modern, well-crafted drinks. "It doesn't take any more effort to make a good Manhattan than a bad one," says St. John Frizell of Fort Defiance. "It takes a bit more care, and that's it. So why shouldn't your neighborhood bar make a really good Manhattan?"

"It doesn't take any more effort to make a good Manhattan than a bad one."

— *St. John Frizell, Fort Defiance*

The Brooklyn bars—and bartenders—profiled in these pages are hardly all of a kind. Some are good-time, elevated dives that dabble in cocktails; others opened when their owners, who themselves ran Williamsburg shot-and-beer bars, sought something more civilized; some were Manhattan trailblazers crossing the river. But from classy pre-Prohibition-style Clover Club and breathtaking *Belle Époque* Maison Premiere to stripped-down, anything-goes Dram and playful, irreverent Extra Fancy, they share two goals—making excellent drinks, and embracing all those who seek to imbibe them.

Tijuana Lady, Fort Defiance

Of course, Brooklyn did not spring into being with the first Williamsburg hipsters, and Hotel Delmano and Huckleberry Bar, while early to the cocktail game, were hardly the first bars in the borough. Brooklyn's bar history is a long and proud one, which could make for its own book—but our focus is on the cocktail culture of the last decade.

In these pages you'll find snapshots of 25 wildly different Brooklyn bars, from elegant establishments whose cocktails attract national—and even international—attention, to friendly dives with formidable whiskey selections, to lesser-known neighborhood favorites. And you'll find recipes by many of Brooklyn's top bartenders themselves from the bars profiled, as well as from many other fine establishments, both restaurants and bars, in the borough.

MAISON PREMIERE

THE ESSENTIALS

Just about any drinker who's been to a craft cocktail bar knows the feeling: that sense of awe as a skilled bartender shakes together ingredients with a signature rhythm, pours a drink that crests right at the top of the coupe, and presents a cocktail as attractive as it will prove delicious. The best cocktails are more than the sum of their parts: They're experiences unto themselves.

How do they pull off this wizardry? Years of practice, to be sure, aided by topflight ingredients, and obsessive attention to everything from garnishes to barware to ice—there's a reason that cocktails from Brooklyn's best bartenders are so exquisite.

But even though at-home bartenders might never *quite* achieve that level—at least, not without hundreds of hours of practice—they can get awfully close. Armed with basic knowledge and equipment, would-be home mixologists can refine their cocktail game, perhaps more quickly than they'd think.

While few of us will ever have the arsenal of spirits and ingredients that the best cocktail bars do, taking the time to learn the basics—and invest in the essential bottles and tools—will make an enormous difference.

INGREDIENTS

10 ESSENTIAL BOTTLES

VODKA

The ultimate blank canvas for flavors, and still the liquor of choice for many. Once you're above the true bottom shelf, most expensive vodkas get their sticker price through marketing, rather than quality. Wodka vodka is a real value; Russian Standard and Tito's are two other favorites.

GIN

The juniper-flavored spirit stars in classic cocktails and 21st-century creations alike. Tanqueray and Beefeater are both excellent, time-tested gins in the classic London Dry style; Plymouth, a little pricier but favored by many bartenders; Greenhall's, a great value. (And if you want to be *truly* Brooklyn, grab a bottle of local Brooklyn Gin or Dorothy Parker.)

LIGHT RUM

Another clear spirit, white rum integrates beautifully with many flavors, and is versatile far beyond its usual uses in mojitos and daiquiris. Brugal Extra Dry will shine in any light rum cocktails, as will Banks 5 Year or El Dorado 3 Year.

BLANCO TEQUILA

Silver tequila is best known for margaritas but has any number of other uses in the cocktail world. Look for the designation "100% agave" when picking out a bottle. Pueblo Viejo and Espolón are widely available and a good value.

BOURBON

American-made and often a touch sweeter than its fellow whiskeys, bourbon is endlessly friendly for mixing. Evan Williams Black Label is an unbeatable value, and Old Grand-Dad, similar. Old Forester is a classic, if slightly pricier, bourbon for those new to the genre.

RYE

Generally spicier and drier than bourbon, rye is the spirit of choice for many bartenders when making classic cocktails—Old Fashioneds and Manhattans among them. Rye is the rare category where there's a true consensus on value and quality; Rittenhouse and Old Overholt are almost universal favorites.

SWEET VERMOUTH

The aromatized wine is essential to Manhattans, Negronis, and every variation thereof. Keep it refrigerated; vermouth is wine-based and will go off just as an open bottle of wine would (if more slowly). Virtually every craft cocktail bartender today will recommend Carpano Antica Formula sweet vermouth; it's a bit pricier than others, so seek out a 375-mL for your first bottle.

DRY VERMOUTH

As essential in the mixology world as its sweeter, darker counterpart. This, too, must be refrigerated once opened. Dolin Dry is an excellent choice here; if it's not available where you are, Noilly Prat is a good alternative.

Tooker Alley

ORANGE LIQUEUR

From the margarita to the Sidecar, orange liqueur is indispensable; Cointreau is your best bet for a versatile midpriced bottle; dry Curaçao is another favorite.

ANGOSTURA BITTERS

When there's just a dash of bitters in any given drink, they may seem optional, but that dash is critical to balance out a cocktail—and when used with a little more gusto, Angostura (or as the pros often call it, Ango) contributes an intriguing element of warm, earthy spice.

...AND 10 MORE

COGNAC

In pre-Prohibition days, brandy was the base spirit of choice for many classic cocktails, and smooth, aged Cognac was considered the best of all. The very word *Cognac* connotes a luxury product, and its price tag is why Cognac cocktails are somewhat rare today; but several houses have released moderately priced, cocktail-friendly bottles developed for mixologists; look for H by Hine or Pierre Ferrand 1840.

BLENDED SCOTCH

While many drinkers sip their Scotch neat or, at the most, with a splash of water, blended Scotches form the base of many excellent cocktails. The Famous Grouse is widely available and a good value.

Hotel Delmano

DARK RUM

Whereas white rum disappears seamlessly into many cocktails, longer-aged rums have a robust, often whiskey-like character all their own. Diplomático Reserva, Ron Zacapa Centenario, and El Dorado 12-Year are all good bets.

REPOSADO TEQUILA

Reposado translates to "rested"; reposado tequila is a lightly aged spirit, "rested" in barrels for up to one year, that's a bit smoother and weightier than its lighter-colored counterparts. Pueblo Viejo is a real value.

MEZCAL

Known to only the most devoted of liquor nerds a few years ago, mezcal is now a bartender favorite across the country. Like tequila, it's a spirit made from agave, but it has a distinct, smoky character. Fidencio Mezcal and Del Maguey Vida are both highly recommended.

IRISH WHISKEY

American-made bourbon and rye are a great start, but Irish whiskey, generally on the lighter and sweeter side, also shines in cocktails. There's nothing wrong with fallback Jameson, though Tullamore D.E.W. is a better value.

CAMPARI

Bright red and utterly unique, this bittersweet amaro stars in classic cocktails (you can't make a Negroni without it!) and any number of bartenders' newer creations.

APEROL

A close cousin of Campari, Aperol is lighter and less bitter, with a compelling orange flavor that brightens many a modern cocktail. (Like Campari, Aperol is a distinct product, rather than a category; there's only one Aperol. Ditto St-Germain, Chartreuse, and Fernet-Branca, to follow.)

MARASCHINO

Not the neon-red liquid in the cherry jar, but a sophisticated cherry-based liqueur that plays a part in many classics. Luxardo maraschino is the gold standard.

ORANGE BITTERS

Between orange and Angostura bitters, you'll have the finishing touch for a huge number of cocktails. (Many companies make orange bitters, including Angostura's orange, which will be the most widely available; Regan's orange bitters are a favorite.)

AND A FEW MORE FOR FUN ...

APPLEJACK

A barrel-aged apple brandy, considered by many to be the "original" American spirit (George Washington was among its fans). It drinks like a slightly sweeter whiskey with a distinct apple character. Laird's is the first—and still the best—producer; their "Bottled in Bond" is the applejack to get, made from nothing but apples.

ST-GERMAIN

A brand of sweet elderflower liqueur that's become tremendously popular in recent years.

FERNET BRANCA

Powerfully bitter and herbal, verging on the medicinal, Fernet is the darling of 21st-century bartenders; it's an acquired taste, to put it mildly.

CHARTREUSE

A distinctive liqueur made by French Carthusian monks since the 18th century. Green Chartreuse is higher-proof and more strongly herbal; yellow Chartreuse, mellower and sweeter, appears more often in cocktails.

PAMPLEMOUSSE

Like fashion or music, cocktails go through trends, and right now this grapefruit liqueur is popping its head up everywhere. Combier is an excellent brand.

AND A FEW MORE BITTERS, ETC. ...

While Angostura and orange bitters will get you far, today's bartenders have dozens, if not hundreds, more to choose from. If you've got room for one more bottle, go with the bright red Peychaud's, with a distinctive anise character, which often appears in classics. Beyond that? Nearly across the board, Brooklyn bartenders love Bittermens Very Small Batch bitters; in this book, you'll find many recipes that use their Xocolatl Mole bitters, inspired by Mexican *mole* sauces and flavored with cacao, cinnamon, and spice; the Hellfire Habanero Shrub is a favorite for delivering heat, and the Hopped Grapefruit bitters, a distinctive citrus bitters with vegetal bitterness from hops.

Bitters at The Narrows

ON SWEETENERS

"I want a cocktail that's not too sweet"; or, "I want this drink, but without simple syrup." Bartenders might hear some version of this every time they're behind the stick. And there are any number of reasons that drinkers are wary of sugar. Up until recently, your average cocktail, made with corn syrup–laden mixers and sugar-filled juices, tended to be very sweet; in most cases, overly so. These drinks turned plenty of would-be drinkers off cocktails altogether. (Calorie-counting plays a role too, although here's a tip: If you're concerned about calories in cocktails, they're not coming from that quarter-ounce of simple syrup. They're coming from the alcohol.)

> **When people say not too sweet—and it happens all the time—there's a bigger conversation we can have ...What does that mean to you?**
>
> — *Liz Stauber, The Narrows*

That said, sweeteners are essential in cocktails. Every well-constructed drink is designed with an eye toward balance—not too spirituous, not too bitter, not too acidic—every flavor in proportion. Taking out the sweetener is like removing one leg from a four-legged stool; the whole thing falls down. Suddenly the sour and bitter and boozy elements are all out of whack. Some cocktails, of course, are sweeter than others, and some drinkers prefer cocktails that are sweeter than others. Plenty of drinks are intended to be powerfully bitter, or spirit-forward, or tart. But it's essential to try a recipe as written, rather than cutting back on the sugar right off the bat. Just as salt in a recipe doesn't necessarily make the dish salty, a sparing amount of sugar doesn't have to make it sweet.

When bartending at home, accept that some sweetener is essential to any cocktail—but beyond that it is a matter of preference. "When people say not too sweet—and it happens all the time—there's a bigger conversation we can have," says Liz Stauber of The Narrows in Bushwick. "What does that mean to you? Did you have a terrible Old Fashioned, where they opened packets of sugar and muddled that with maraschino cherries? Or are you saying that you like something dry and spirit-forward?" There's a cocktail suited to every taste—but regardless of the ingredients, balance is key.

MAKE YOUR OWN
GRENADINE

RECIPE: GRENADINE

4 oz/120 mL 100% pomegranate
juice, fresh or store-bought
(POM is a good brand)
4 oz/115 g white sugar

In a small saucepan, combine
pomegranate juice and sugar.
Cook over high heat, stirring
gently, until sugar is dissolved
Once it reaches a boil, turn down
to a bare simmer and let cook,
stirring occasionally, for 15 minutes,
until visibly thickened. Let cool to
room temperature before using.

Envision grenadine, and you're probably flashing back to Shirley Temples made with bright-red syrup, cloying enough to satisfy a childhood sweet tooth. But real grenadine is something else altogether. Essentially a reduced pomegranate syrup, it's a classic cocktail ingredient that's worth every minute it takes to make—especially since, once prepared, grenadine will last for weeks in the refrigerator.

Grenadine takes well to experimentation; it can be spiced with whole cloves or cinnamon sticks (add to simmering liquid, then strain out before using), or given a floral character with a few drops of orange flower water. Some modern bars even have secret formulas they won't divulge. Developing your own recipe is half the fun.

*The Improved Pendennis Club Cocktail,
Long Island Bar*

SIMPLE SYRUP

While simple syrup isn't the only way to sweeten a cocktail, it's by far the most common. Whereas putting granulated sugar straight into a drink will result in gritty sugar grains left behind, simple syrup—which is nothing more than white sugar dissolved in an equal amount of hot water—already has the sugar in solution, so it integrates seamlessly.

These days, you'll see simple syrup sold, premade, in supermarkets and gourmet shops. It's a brilliant marketing scheme if ever there were one—combine sugar and water, sell at an obscene markup!—but a huge waste of money and packaging; making simple syrup is as easy, and as quick, as boiling water.

TO MAKE SIMPLE SYRUP

Start with equal parts white sugar and hot water (whether from a kettle, heated in the microwave, or straight from a very hot tap). Stir together until the sugar disappears and the solution is clear. Store in the refrigerator.

... AND OTHERS

Rich simple syrup, two parts sugar to one part water, is preferred by some bartenders, as it contributes less water to a cocktail for a given amount of sugar. You'll also find recipes calling for *demerara syrup*, made with richer, more flavorful demerara sugar; *agave syrup*, well-suited to tequila and mezcal drinks, two spirits that are themselves distilled from agave; and *honey* and *maple syrup*, each a bit richer in body than simple syrup and, of course, each contributing a distinctive flavor.

Recipes without any syrups at all will generally have some other sweet element, whether vermouth, a liqueur like Cointreau or maraschino, or fresh fruit.

RECIPE NOTE
ON SYRUP SPECS

Some bartenders make their honey syrup with equal parts honey and hot water, others 2:1 or 3:1; ditto agave, demerara, and more. For all sweeteners other than simple syrup, the ratio of sweetener to water will be noted in parentheses.

Examples: Rich simple syrup (2:1) denotes 2 parts sugar dissolved in 1 part water; honey syrup (3:1), 3 parts honey to 1 part water; demerara syrup (1:1), equal parts.

ON CITRUS

If there's a single, indisputable rule for making the best cocktails, it might be this: Use fresh juice. *Not* lime juice from concentrate, not from one of those lime-shaped plastic bottles, but from honest-to-goodness limes, squeezed right before you make your cocktails.

The vibrancy and flavor of fresh juice just can't be matched. Citrus juice is perishable, so best used the day it's squeezed. With your trusty hand juicer, making juice won't take more than a minute, and the results will speak for themselves.

FEAR NOT THE
INFUSION!

Nothing sounds more elaborate than a cocktail with "house-infused vodka," or "house-made clove bourbon." Despite the fancy name, the process is generally quite straightforward. Here's the best translation of "infuse": *Place X ingredient in Y spirit. Let sit. Strain.* And you're done.

It's one of the simplest, most powerful ways to up your cocktail game. Bonus: Once you've got a bottle of jalapeño tequila or thyme-infused gin or clove bourbon around, you'll be tempted to experiment with it more and more.

For recipes for infusions, see page 264-270.

Dram

Bar tools, Quarter Bar

EQUIPMENT

As with any craft, proper tools are essential to bartending. And while the mixologists of today might have all manner of wonky gadgets at their disposal—from centrifuges to carbon dioxide chargers to custom ice machines—the basic equipment you need is simple and inexpensive.

ESSENTIAL EQUIPMENT

SHAKER

While any shaker will work, a set of two metal shaking tins is the industry standard. No caps to lose, easy to clean, almost impossible to break.

STRAINER

A "Hawthorne" strainer, with a handle and a spring coiled around the front, will fit neatly over your shaking tin, straining out ice as you pour your finished cocktail.

CITRUS JUICER

Fresh citrus juice is essential to a huge percentage of cocktails; a two-handled "bee-hive" juicer will make quick work of lemons, limes, and more.

MIXING GLASS

While a pint glass will do in a pinch, a proper mixing glass is ideal for stirred cocktails; its volume allows for plenty of ice to chill down the drink.

BAR SPOON

A long-handled bar spoon is designed for stirring cocktails.

JIGGER

What's the use of a cocktail recipe if you're not following the specs? Use a jigger to properly measure your ingredients. ¼ oz/10 mL, ½ oz/15 mL, ¾ oz/20 mL, 1 oz/30 mL, and 2 oz/60 mL are the key measurements; make sure that your jigger (or set of jiggers) has these demarcations.

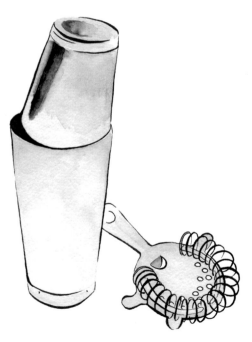

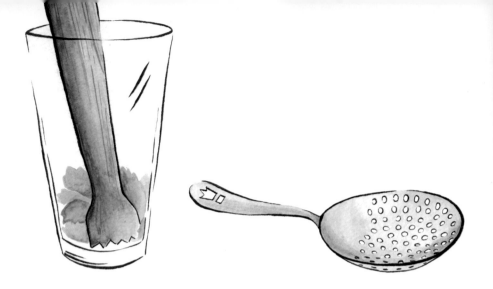

NEXT-LEVEL EQUIPMENT

MUDDLER

A heavy, blunt tool intended for muddling—that is, smashing—tougher fruits, vegetables, and other ingredients.

FINE-MESH STRAINER

For cocktails that require double-straining, generally to remove fine bits of fruit or herbs.

JULEP STRAINER

Generally best for straining out stirred drinks, the julep strainer has a bowl-shaped cup that nestles inside a mixing glass.

SPECIALTY ICE TRAYS

Ice is a key ingredient in every cocktail; high-quality ice trays are worth the investment. 1¼-inch/30-mm cubes are ideal for shaking, while pouring a drink over a single 2- or 2½-inch/70-mm cube (also called "big ice" or "a rock") is an elegant way to present a cocktail in a rocks glass.

PEELER

A sharp knife will work to cut citrus peels for garnishes, but a Y-shaped peeler makes the job easier.

ESSENTIAL GLASSWARE

COUPE
The quintessential cocktail glass, with a wide bowl and thin stem. Used to serve cocktails "up"—that is, without ice.

ROCKS GLASS
Short and squat, for cocktails "on the rocks" (served with ice). An "old fashioned" glass is a smaller version, while a "double old fashioned" is essentially the same as a rocks glass (capacity is the only difference).

FLUTE
For champagne and many sparkling cocktails.

COLLINS GLASS
Tall and straight-sided, named for the Tom Collins—lemon juice, gin, sugar, and soda—but ideal for any long drink (with a large volume of mixer, like soda or tonic). A highball glass is a slightly smaller version.

NEXT-LEVEL

PINT GLASS
For beer, and for (increasingly popular) beer cocktails.

MARTINI GLASS
While a coupe is an elegant way to present a Martini, some drinkers still prefer the V-shaped Martini glass.

JULEP CUPS
Silver-plated cups, filled to the brim and above with crushed ice, are the only proper way to present a julep. Bonus points for matching metal straws.

AND MORE...
Bartenders will use capacious hurricane glasses for tiki-style drinks with crushed ice; copper Moscow Mule mugs for the popular vodka–ginger ale drink; and Nick and Nora glasses for up drinks, an elegant vessel looking like something between a coupe and a small wine glass.

TECHNIQUE

SHAKING VS. STIRRING

As a general rule, *shake* a cocktail any time there's citrus juice, fruit, eggs, or cream; *stir* a cocktail if it has none of the above, meaning the drink is made up of spirits, sweeteners, and modifiers like vermouth.

Why? Drinks with juices need stronger agitation to properly integrate the ingredients, whereas a simple stir will suffice for spirits and the like. Shaking will also turn a drink cloudy, which in the case of a Manhattan or Martini-style drink, sullies its elegant clarity. (Nearly every modern-day cocktail bartender will stir a Martini, rather than shake it; James Bond's catchphrase doesn't quite hold up.)

Either technique achieves two goals. The first, and most obvious, is to chill the drink, so that it's at a proper temperature whether or not it's poured over additional ice. The second? To provide a bit of dilution. As you shake or stir, the ice will begin to melt, and that water will help open up the spirits, integrate the flavors, and temper the alcohol just a bit. If your Negroni or Old Fashioned tastes a little too harsh and boozy, try stirring longer.

HOW TO SHAKE

Add your ingredients to the smaller tin of your shaker. Fill the larger tin about half-full with ice. Pour the contents of the small shaker into the big shaker, nestle the small tin inside the larger one, and pound them together *hard* to get a good seal. Then shake vigorously, really getting your biceps into it. Imagine all the ice ricocheting back and forth, from one end of the shaker to the other—not gently sliding along the bottom. After 10 to 15 seconds you'll feel the shaker getting frosty; that's when you're done.

HOW TO STIR

Fill a mixing glass about 2/3 of the way full with ice, add your ingredients, and stir with a long-handled bar spoon for at least 15 seconds. Experienced bartenders manage a consistent stir while barely moving their hands; visualize the back of the spoon circling around the inside edge of the mixing glass, rather than swiping through the middle. (The motion takes some time to master, but once you do, you'll look like a pro.)

MUDDLING

Some ingredients that aren't already in liquid form—say, cucumber slices, or fresh ginger—require a bit of muscle to release their flavors. That's when bartenders "muddle," which essentially translates to "smash up." Generally, the ingredient will be put in the bottom of a cocktail shaker, where it'll get a few hard smashes with a muddler, before the other ingredients are added and it's all shaken together.

The Richardson

THE "DRY SHAKE" AND "WET SHAKE" (ADVANCED!)

It's rare that you'll shake ingredients together without ice, with one exception: When you're using egg. Egg white is a classic cocktail ingredient; when shaken together with liquids, it develops a frothy, silky texture (but, don't worry, doesn't make the drink taste "eggy" at all). You'll also see drinks that call for whole eggs, though today that's less common.

In order to properly fluff up the egg white, bartenders generally "dry shake": Combine all the ingredients in a shaker, and shake *without* ice for 8 to 10 seconds. Then they add ice and shake again to chill and further combine; that's the "wet shake."

GARNISH LIKE A PRO

It's easy to assume that garnishes are optional—after all, the *real* cocktail is what's in the glass, right? But most garnishes are far more than ornamental. (Excluding cocktail umbrellas, which are just plain fun.) When a Martini gets a "twist" of lemon, it's not only for the aesthetics: Twisting a strip of lemon peel over the glass releases citrus oils, leaving a thin sheen on the surface of the cocktail. What we perceive as the taste of a drink is inextricably linked to its scent, and these garnishes contribute essential aromas.

HOW TO GARNISH WITH HERBS

Whether you're working with mint, rosemary, basil, or other herbs, there are a few cardinal rules: Make sure the herbs are clean, fresh, and cosmetically appealing (nothing lowers expectations for a drink like a wilted garnish). For rosemary, that means a long, intact stem; for basil and mint, choose the best-looking sprig, where several leaves are still attached.

Before garnishing with herbs, bartenders will slap them lightly against their palms. Why? It helps to release their aromatic oils. Do a quick test: Take a whiff of a few basil leaves; then slap them against your palm and sniff again. The scent will be much more powerful the second time around.

One More That's It, Extra Fancy

HOW TO MAKE A TWIST

For a lemon, orange, grapefruit, or lime twist, use a sharp paring knife or vegetable peeler to cut a long, thin slice of peel—at least an inch and a half long, and half an inch wide. Try to get mostly the colored peel, avoiding the white pith as much as possible.

After your cocktail is poured into the glass, finish with the twist: Hold it by both edges over the surface of the drink, colored side down, and quickly pull the edges up and together, to spritz its oils over the cocktail. (If you've done it right, you'll smell citrus immediately, and with clear cocktails, you should be able to see a thin sheen on the drink's surface.) Some bartenders will then lightly rub the twist around the rim of the cocktail glass to further distribute its oils before dropping it in. (Generally a twist is left in the cocktail, but in some cases only the oils are desired, and the peel itself is discarded.)

HOW TO MAKE A FLAMING TWIST (ADVANCED!)

Most bartenders (and most bar-goers) love a dramatic presentation—and nothing is quite as dramatic as fire. Citrus oils are flammable, so catching them with a flame as they're sprayed over a drink causes a quick burst of fire. A proper flaming twist will give your drink a powerful, smoky aroma, and give your audience quite a show, though it's difficult to pull off. This is a trick best attempted in a sober state, well clear of anything else that's flammable.

Instructions: Make a nice, big citrus peel (generally orange or grapefruit), according to the directions above; the longer and broader it is, the bigger the flame you're likely to get. Over the surface of the drink, hold the peel (colored side down) in one hand, and a lighter in the other. Pass the flame several times back and forth over the peel, warming it up, before holding the flame right under the peel and spritzing the citrus oils over the drink—if you've aimed correctly and made a proper peel, you should be rewarded with a burst of flame.

HAVE FUN WITH IT

"Functional garnishes are ideal, but sometimes a garnish can be about pure aesthetics," says Will Elliott of Maison Premiere. In other words, presentation matters. "I believe, elementally, that the visual is right alongside all the other senses for enjoying cocktails. Everything plays a part in enjoying the drink."

10
Steps to Instantly Improve
YOUR COCKTAILS

1. SHAKE LONG AND HARD.

As we've discussed, shaking doesn't just mix ingredients together; it chills them thoroughly and, just as important, allows a bit of ice melt, water that helps a cocktail open up and express its flavors. A professional bartender will always appreciate a powerful shake. (The same principle applies to stirring.)

2. TAKE ICE SERIOUSLY.

If you're using ice that has been in your freezer for months, it'll taste like everything *else* that's been in your freezer for months. And if that ice is chipped and beaten up, it'll dilute a drink more quickly than you'll want, watering it down. Invest in high-quality trays for uniform, well-formed ice cubes.

3. GARNISH LIKE A PRO.

Citrus peels should be long, relatively free of pith, and properly spritzed over the top of the drink; herbs should be clean, attractive, and lightly slapped against your hand to release their oils.

4. SET UP YOUR "MISE EN PLACE."

Borrowed from the culinary world, the term *mise en place* refers to your setup—ingredients neatly laid out before your hands get anywhere near a shaker. If you've got simple syrup, fresh-squeezed juice, spirits, and proper garnishes all at the ready, shaking a cocktail will be a snap, just as it is for a professional bartender. If, on the other hand, you're scrambling to find the bourbon while you're halfway through mixing the other ingredients, the process becomes far more disorganized.

5. REFRIGERATE YOUR VERMOUTH.

Most of the people out there who don't like vermouth haven't tried it fresh; if they use vermouth at all, they've had the same dusty bottle hidden in a cabinet for a decade or more. Vermouth should be refrigerated, and ideally consumed within a few weeks after opening; end of story. "Buy a little 375-mL bottle of vermouth, just to keep it fresh," recommends Joel Lee Kulp of The Richardson.

6. SQUEEZE YOUR JUICES FRESH.

Lemon juice from concentrate bears little resemblance to fresh-squeezed lemon; ditto all other citrus. If you're taking the time to make a craft cocktail, take the extra 30 seconds to make fresh juice.

7. BITTERS ARE YOUR FRIEND.

Some bartenders call bitters the "salt and pepper" of the culinary world—flavoring agents that transform a drink. To start, invest in orange and Angostura bitters, available at most liquor stores and grocery stores. A single bottle will last a good long time, and prove itself to be a worthwhile investment with all the well-balanced cocktails you'll make.

8. SO IS SIMPLE SYRUP.

Sweetening ingredients in cocktails, whether simple syrup, honey, or liqueurs, aren't used with the intention of making a drink sweet, as such. Rather, they create balance and bind other flavors together. All recipes in this book result in sophisticated, balanced cocktails; don't assume, if you don't have a sweet tooth, that the sugar should be dialed down.

9. INVEST IN GOOD INGREDIENTS.

Why buy a $15 bottle of gin instead of a $20 one, if the former results in subpar cocktails and the latter will yield some excellent drinks? Spirits differ dramatically in quality, and "more expensive" doesn't always translate to "better"; that said, stay away from the true bottom shelf; you'll thank yourself later.

10. GET TO KNOW YOUR JIGGER.

Craft bartenders are precise in their measurements; ¼ ounce of orange liqueur in a cocktail might not register at all, whereas ½ ounce is exactly what's needed. So make sure that you're following recipes faithfully by taking the time to measure. Yes, experienced bartenders often "free-pour" without jiggers, eyeballing each ingredient—but they've spent hundreds upon hundreds of hours practicing that ability. My advice: Leave the free-pouring to the pros and trust in your jigger.

Is any other spirit so perfectly suited to cocktails as gin?

While you do find the occasional diehard juniperphile who will sip the stuff neat, gin virtually always appears in cocktail form—from simple G&Ts, to Martinis and Gimlets, to far more elaborate creations conceived in this century or in centuries past.

To understand gin's affinity for the cocktail, it's important to understand how the spirit is made. "At the end of the day, gin is just flavored vodka," says Joel Lee Kulp. It's a line favored by many modern bartenders as a different perspective on gin. A base of neutral spirit is flavored and redistilled with a host of botanicals—juniper prime among them, which gives gin its characteristic piney scent.

Other ingredients generally include citrus peel, coriander, angelica root, and orris root, and spices like cinnamon, cardamom, and nutmeg. Thus gin has an affinity for fruit flavors, since gin itself has a citrus element; and an affinity for herbal flavors, whether fresh herbs or an herbal liqueur or vermouth.

Until recently, American liquor stores showcased primarily British gins. And while the major players (Beefeater, Tanqueray, Bombay) are still imported, the last decade

GIN

has seen an explosion in gins on the market, with craft distillers now numbering in the hundreds.

From a logistical standpoint, gin is one of the fastest spirits to produce—there's no waiting around for spirits to mature (as with whiskey, many brandies and rums, and others), and no associated costs of barrels and warehouses. Redistill a neutral grain spirit with an array of botanicals, include enough juniper, and you've got gin.

But it's that blend of botanicals that makes every gin different—and makes the category endlessly fascinating. "The pleasure of gin is, each one is wholly original," says Allen Katz of New York Distilling Co., which produces three different gins (among other spirits). "With every bottle, you can say, this is what makes mine unique—and this is how I would use it in a cocktail."

It's the bartender's job to understand the nuanced flavors in their gins of choice, and then finesse them accordingly, whether preparing a straightforward Martini or a more complicated invention. "I love it when people sit down at the bar and tell me, 'I don't drink gin'," says Kulp—so he can persuade them otherwise. "I want to find your gateway drug, the cocktail that can make you appreciate gin. And I'd tell a customer, don't overthink it—just try this drink, I think you'll love it. And know that it's gin."

THE RICHARDSON

With gold brocade wallpaper and smartly attired bartenders, The Richardson, opened in 2008, resembled few other places in its out-of-the-way corner of North Williamsburg. But owner Joel Lee Kulp didn't want a feeling of formality. "I didn't want people to think this was some fancy bar," he says. "It's not *fancy*—but it's nice. You should feel good coming in. We clean it! We dress properly! We know how to speak to you about cocktails!"

Proper, professional, and knowledgeable—yet approachable, comfortable, and fun—was Kulp's mantra. He took the leap into bar ownership after more than a decade working in the bar world, while also pursuing work as a filmmaker. He had lived in Williamsburg for years, so the neighborhood was an obvious choice. "I explored other neighborhoods but it didn't feel right," says Kulp. "I understand the nuance in this part of town, and how it's different from one block to the next."

The beginning was an exciting time, he remembers; nearby drinking options were limited, and the neighborhood welcomed a well-run cocktail bar with open arms. "People would walk in, look left and right, and say: *Thank you.*" The Richardson soon became a local fixture—over the years, it's hosted everything from wedding receptions to birthday parties for customers' children. "We have regulars who have been coming in since Day 1," says Kulp. Some of these relationships turned professional: The current general manager started out as a regular, as did a longtime senior bartender.

While the cocktail list leans heavily on the classics, bartenders are constantly experimenting. "We talk about ideas, do tastings together, try new products . . . it's not about mining the cocktail books to find the most esoteric recipes."

"We don't think of the bartenders as the keepers of all these secrets that nobody can know," says Kulp. "When you're at the bar, they should make you feel comfortable enough to ask questions: *I've never had this before, what is this ingredient, what does it taste like?* So you come out the other end knowing something you didn't before."

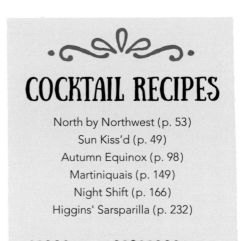

COCKTAIL RECIPES

North by Northwest (p. 53)
Sun Kiss'd (p. 49)
Autumn Equinox (p. 98)
Martiniquais (p. 149)
Night Shift (p. 166)
Higgins' Sarsparilla (p. 232)

❝ When you're at the bar, they should make you feel comfortable enough to ask questions ... So you come out the other end knowing something you didn't before. ❞

— Joel Lee Kulp, The Richardson

San Francisco Handshake, Hotel Delmano

SAN FRANCISCO HANDSHAKE

Sam Anderson, Hotel Delmano

Herbaceous on its own, gin takes particularly well to herbal flavors, like the fresh thyme used in this longtime favorite from Hotel Delmano. Bitter, herbal Fernet-Branca—the bartender's shot of choice in Brooklyn, but even more so in San Francisco—gave this cocktail its name; a shared Fernet shot is known as a "bartender's handshake."

1½ oz/45 mL thyme-infused gin (recipe p. 265)
¾ oz/20 mL lemon juice
¾ oz/20 mL St-Germain
½ oz/15 mL simple syrup
¼ oz/10 mL Fernet-Branca

Combine all the ingredients in a cocktail shaker with ice. Shake until well chilled and strain into a chilled coupe. Garnish with a thyme sprig.

WATERSHIP DOWN

Jeremy Oertel, Donna

Gin can tack toward sweet or savory with equal ease; celery and ginger leave this tall drink dry and refreshing.

1½ oz/45 mL Dorothy Parker American gin
1 oz/30 mL Dolin dry vermouth
¾ oz/20 mL lime juice
½ oz/15 mL ginger syrup (recipe p. 273)
2 dashes Bittermens Orchard Street
  Celery Shrub
Club soda

Combine all the ingredients except the soda in a cocktail shaker with ice. Shake until well chilled and strain into a Collins glass with fresh ice. Top with club soda. Garnish with a long celery stalk.

TRANS-SIBERIAN

Damon Boelte, Grand Army

Building from a pairing of gin and citrus, Aperol contributes a vibrant hue, and orange flower water, a slight floral note.

1½ oz/45 mL gin
½ oz/15 mL Aperol
½ oz/15 mL lime juice
½ oz/15 mL grapefruit juice
¼ oz/10 mL simple syrup
1 drop orange flower water
Pinch of sea salt

Combine all the ingredients in a cocktail shaker with ice. Shake until well chilled and strain into a coupe. Garnish with a grapefruit twist.

ROSEMARY'S BABY

Lurie De La Rosa-Jackson, Do or Dine

Gin and rosemary are an intuitive pairing, shaken here with lemon and with pear juice to add body and sweetness. Great for novice gin drinkers who want something herbal, but not overwhelmingly so.

2 oz/60 mL Gordon's gin
¾ oz/20 mL rosemary syrup (recipe p. 277)
¾ oz/20 mL lemon juice
½ oz/15 mL Goya pear juice

Combine all the ingredients in a cocktail shaker with ice. Shake until well chilled and strain into a highball glass with fresh ice. Garnish with a rosemary sprig.

I'LL HAVE WHAT SHE'S HAVING

Ian Hardie, Huckleberry Bar

Some drinks are just easy to love, as is this well-named cocktail from Huckleberry Bar; any bartender could eyeball this recipe and tell you it'll be an easy sell.

1½ oz/45 mL gin
¾ oz/20 mL lemon juice
½ oz/15 mL St-Germain
½ oz/15 mL Aperol
2 dashes Peychaud's bitters

Combine all the ingredients in a cocktail shaker with ice. Shake until well chilled and double-strain into a coupe. Garnish with a grapefruit twist.

GIN BLOSSOM

Julie Reiner, Clover Club

A house classic whose reputation now transcends Clover Club, this Martini variation brings in apricot liqueur to play off the dry, herbal gin and vermouth pairing.

1½ oz/45 mL Plymouth gin
1½ oz/45 mL Martini bianco dry vermouth
¾ oz/20 mL apricot eau-de-vie
2 dashes orange bitters

Combine all the ingredients in a mixing glass with ice. Stir until well chilled and strain into a Nick and Nora glass. Garnish with an orange twist.

Gin Blossom, Clover Club

TAKES ON THE
MARTINI

There are as many ways to make a Martini as there are bartenders stirring them. And as Liz Stauber of The Narrows notes, "Martinis are the rare drink where just about everyone who orders one knows what they want." While dirty vodka Martinis are still many bar-goers' drink of choice, most of today's Brooklyn bartenders prefer gin, hold back on the olive brine, and bring in more than a whisper of vermouth. Here are five takes on the much-loved classic.

KEITH KENJI COCHRAN
THE NARROWS

"A nice, snappy martini. It's got an herbal backbone and it's clean and crisp, awesome with a plate of oysters."

2½ oz/75 mL Bar Hill gin
½ oz/15 mL Dolin
dry vermouth
1 dash orange bitters

Combine all the ingredients in a mixing glass with ice. Stir until well chilled and strain into a chilled coupe or martini glass. Garnish with a lemon twist.

JOEL LEE KULP
THE RICHARDSON

"I've always wanted to like olives in my martini, but it's never happened. I go with a lemon twist or an onion instead."

2 oz/60 mL Beefeater gin
1 oz/30 mL Dolin
dry vermouth

Combine all the ingredients in a mixing glass with ice. Stir until well chilled and strain into a chilled coupe or Martini glass. Garnish with a lemon twist or an onion.

TOM MACY
CLOVER CLUB

"I'd love to see people drinking classic martinis again. I don't understand the aversion to dry vermouth. All it adds is flavor."

2 oz/60 mL Tanqueray 10 gin
1 oz/30 mL Dolin
dry vermouth
1 dash orange bitters

Combine all the ingredients in a mixing glass with ice. Stir until well chilled and strain into a chilled coupe. Garnish with a lemon twist.

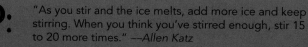

PRO TIP: "As you stir and the ice melts, add more ice and keep stirring. When you think you've stirred enough, stir 15 to 20 more times." —Allen Katz

ST. JOHN FRIZELL
FORT DEFIANCE

2¼ oz/70 mL Plymouth Gin
¾ oz/20 mL Dolin Dry vermouth
1 dash orange bitters

Combine all the ingredients in a mixing glass with ice. Stir until well chilled and strain into a coupe. Garnish with a lemon twist.

ALLEN KATZ
NEW YORK DISTILLING COMPANY

"Perry's Tot is a traditional dry gin, so I use a fruit-forward vermouth like Dolin blanc. Grapefruit is a minor botanical in the gin, thus the garnish."

1½ oz/45 mL Perry's Tot Navy Strength gin
1½ oz/45 mL Dolin blanc vermouth
1 dash orange bitters

Combine all the ingredients in a mixing glass with ice. Stir until well chilled and strain into a chilled coupe or martini glass. Garnish with a grapefruit twist.

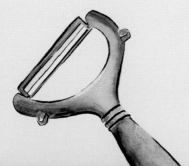

ALICE'S MALLET
David Moo, Quarter Bar

"This is one of my favorite cocktails," says Moo, who stews rhubarb into a compote that he then strains for a tart, viscous syrup that comes alive with lemon, gin, and Aperol.

2 oz/60 mL Plymouth gin
1 oz/30 mL rhubarb syrup (recipe p. 276)
1 scant tsp orgeat syrup
1 tsp Aperol
1 tsp lemon juice
1 dash Regan's No. 6 orange bitters

Combine all the ingredients in a cocktail shaker with ice. Shake until well chilled and strain into a chilled coupe.

CLOVER CLUB
Clover Club

The namesake cocktail at this much-loved Carroll Gardens bar is a classic that's hard to resist. "Back when cocktail drinkers were just getting into gin, I used to have this on the menu as a crossover drink from vodka, like a "money-back guarantee" if you didn't like it—if you're not a fan, I'll make you a Cosmo," says Julie Reiner. "Only a handful of drinks are this likable. It's fruity and frothy and delicious."

1½ oz/45 mL Plymouth gin
½ oz/15 mL dry vermouth
½ oz/15 mL lemon juice
½ oz/15 mL raspberry syrup (recipe p. 274)
¼ oz/10 mL egg white

Combine all the ingredients in a cocktail shaker without ice. Shake vigorously for a "dry shake," then add ice and shake again. Strain into a coupe. Garnish with a raspberry.

Sauvetage and Cannibal Corpse Reviver #2, The Shanty

BROOKLYN SLING

John Bush, Talde

The Singapore Sling dates back to the early 20th century and has evolved considerably since; today's recipes might contain pineapple, cherry brandy, Benedictine, grenadine, or any combination thereof. John Bush's version is strong on the Broker's London dry gin, with Luxardo maraschino and a bit of high-quality grenadine.

2 oz/60 mL Broker's gin
2 oz/60 mL pineapple juice
½ oz/15 mL lime juice
¼ oz/10 mL Luxardo maraschino
3 dashes Angostura bitters
2 dashes grenadine (recipe p. 19)

Combine all the ingredients in a cocktail shaker with ice. Shake until well chilled and strain into a half-pint glass with fresh ice. Garnish with a lime wheel.

SAUVETAGE

Nate Dumas, The Shanty

Though only ½ ounce is called for, Bittermens Amer Sauvage is at the core of this drink—a powerfully bitter American-made liqueur flavored with gentian root, an ingredient used in bitters and herbal French aperitifs. Vermouth, gin, and grapefruit gently echo the bitter complexity.

1 oz/30 mL Dorothy Parker American gin
1 oz/30 mL Carpano Antica Formula
  sweet vermouth
½ oz/15 mL grapefruit juice
½ oz/15 mL Bittermens Amer Sauvage

Combine all the ingredients in a cocktail shaker with ice. Shake until well chilled and double-strain into a chilled coupe. Garnish with an orange twist.

CANNIBAL CORPSE REVIVER #2

Nate Dumas, The Shanty

The classic Corpse Reviver #2 makes use of Cointreau and Lillet, with a dash of absinthe; Nate Dumas's version from The Shanty balances the formidable power of 114-proof Navy Strength gin with pear eau-de-vie and Prosecco—with a teaspoon of Fernet to keep things interesting.

1½ oz/45 mL Perry's Tot Navy Strength gin
½ oz/15 mL lemon juice
½ oz/15 mL simple syrup
4 dashes pear eau-de-vie
1 tsp/5 mL Fernet-Branca
Prosecco

Combine all the ingredients except the Prosecco in a cocktail shaker with ice. Shake until well chilled and strain into a Collins glass filled with fresh ice. Top with Prosecco and garnish with a thin lemon wheel. Serve with a straw.

CLASSIC CORPSE REVIVER #2

Gin, orange liqueur, and light aperitif Lillet in perfect proportion.

1 oz/30 mL gin
1 oz/30 mL Cointreau
1 oz/30 mL Lillet
1 oz/30 mL lemon juice
Absinthe

Add a small amount of absinthe to a coupe glass and turn to coat the inside of the glass; discard excess liquid. In a mixing glass with ice, stir together the remaining ingredients until well chilled. Strain into the prepared coupe and garnish with an orange twist.

HUCKLEBERRY BAR

"Here's how I introduce the bar to people who don't know us: We are the representation of craft cocktails in this neighborhood," says Ian Hardie, beverage director of Huckleberry Bar on Williamsburg's Grand Street. "We were one of the first bars on this street, let alone cocktail bars."

Back in 2007, the cocktail landscape, and the Williamsburg landscape, looked far different. "This street was pretty desolate," says Hardie. But from their first days, the Huckleberry team set the bar high, crafting ambitious cocktail lists—up to 30 cocktails per menu, rotating four times each year. "The intention with every list is to create new cocktails that introduce new flavors, new ideas, new aspects of creativity."

Some of those cocktails are elegant but straightforward, like the gin, Aperol, and St-Germain "I'll Have What She's Having"; others a bit more boundary-pushing, like the "Drinking at the Gym," pairing bourbon with a spiced red bell pepper syrup. "It's a collection of sweet, savory, and citrusy elements; it's one of the drinks that violates your comfort zone a little." But, notes Hardie, it's also one of their bestsellers. "That's really the goal—to make something new that's also well-received."

Like so many Brooklyn bars, Huckleberry quickly won a crowd of die-hard locals ("I've been seeing some of the faces for eight years," says Hardie) and then earned a reputation beyond the immediate neighborhood. "We get a lot of dates, Internet dates especially; then on the weekends, we bring in a DJ, and it's a much more intense, festive mood."

But regardless of its popularity or the sophistication of the cocktails, Hardie wants Huckleberry Bar to remain approachable. "The idea has always been to look nice but not stuffy," Hardie says of his bartenders' look, and the bar as a whole. "Out here on Grand Street you can't really be stuffy. That just doesn't work for the neighborhood. No one wants that. *I* don't want that."

COCKTAIL RECIPES

I'll Have What She's Having (p. 39)
Drinking at the Gym (p. 104)
Faith and Fortitude (p. 111)
Sampogna (p. 174)

**" We are the representation of craft
cocktails in this neighborhood ... We were
one of the first bars on this street, let
alone cocktail bars. "**

—Ian Hardie, Huckleberry Bar

ON "BARTENDER'S CHOICE"

These days, many craft cocktail bars have menus with a dozen or more drinks to choose from. But some guests choose to go off-menu entirely, asking the bartender to devise something on the spot, with a few guidelines. Call it "bartender's choice."

Some bars actively encourage the practice, going to far as to note it on the menu; others would rather stick to their tried-and-true cocktails. It's a polarizing topic between bars, and even individual bartenders. A bartender who would rather not be named told me about working at a "bespoke" cocktail bar, every drink designed on the spot. Ingredients, generally fruits and herbs, were listed out on the menu, and cocktail orders inevitably "turned into a Jamba Juice," as he put it. (Strawberry, *and* mango, *and* mint?)

"There can be more misunderstandings than successes," says Liz Stauber of The Narrows. "A lot of times you really have to take the time to talk about what people like and want, to really draw that information out of them"—which can be difficult to manage on a Friday night.

> **So many times that's where our next cocktail ideas come from.**
> —Ian Hardie, Huckleberry Bar

But Ian Hardie of Huckleberry Bar, which has upward of 30 cocktails on the menu, encourages the practice nonetheless. "Out of the exploration and creativity in 'bartender's choice,' so many times that's where our next cocktail ideas come from," he says. "Here's the best test of a good cocktail: You make it for somebody, they drink it, they like it, they pay for it. Rather than having bartenders sitting down and overanalyzing every ingredient. I'd rather know what the layperson thinks."

Ian Hardie, Huckleberry Bar

The Arnaud Palmer, Loosie Rouge

VIOLET BEAUREGARDE

Katherine Pangaro, No. 7

Blueberries macerated in sugar and a hint of anise-forward liqueur Pernod lend distinct character to this otherwise straightforward cocktail.

2 oz/60 mL gin
½ oz/15 mL lemon juice
½ oz/15 mL simple syrup
2 Tbsp macerated blueberries (see below)
Club soda

In the bottom of a cocktail shaker, muddle the macerated blueberries and lemon juice. Add the gin and simple syrup, then add a few ice cubes and shake until well chilled. Pour the entire cocktail, including ice, into a rocks glass. Top with club soda.

MACERATED BLUEBERRIES: In a quart-size container, toss together ½ pint/475 mL of blueberries, ¼ cup/240 mL of sugar, and 1 oz/30 mL of Pernod. Refrigerate for at least 30 minutes before using.

ARNAUD PALMER

Arnaud Dissais, Loosie Rouge

This punny twist on the iced tea-lemonade "Arnold Palmer" is named for its creator, Arnaud Dissais. Gin, hibiscus tea, bitter Cynar, and sweet sherry and cassis come together for a tall drink with a pleasant, slightly bitter tea backbone with tart and floral elements alongside.

1 oz/30 mL Citadelle gin
½ oz/15 mL Cynar
½ oz/15 mL Lillet Rouge
½ oz/15 mL Pedro Ximénez
½ oz/15 mL Lejay crème de cassis
½ oz/15 mL lemon juice
2 oz/60 mL hibiscus tea

Combine all the ingredients in a cocktail shaker with ice. Shake until well chilled and strain into a Collins glass with fresh ice.

SUN KISS'D

The Richardson

Whereas the classic Negroni (gin, Campari, sweet vermouth) is powerfully bitter, The Richardson's version lightens things up with gently herbal aperitif wines Cappelletti and Cocchi Americano and the light, aromatic Del Professore vermouth.

1½ oz/45 mL Plymouth gin
½ oz/15 mL Cappelletti
½ oz/15 mL Cocchi Americano
½ oz/15 mL del Professore vermouth

Combine all the ingredients in a mixing glass with ice. Stir until well chilled and strain into a chilled coupe.

NEW YORK DISTILLING CO.

When Allen Katz and his two partners first had the idea for New York Distilling Co., they knew from the beginning that their distillery would be in Brooklyn. "We wanted a city-centric distillery," Katz says, "so we could invite people in to observe distillation, both consumers and industry. So they can learn about an activity that they might think only happens in Kentucky, or in Europe."

Occupying an industrial building in a corner of Williamsburg bordering Greenpoint, New York Distilling Co. now produces gins and rye whiskeys sold nationally and internationally.

From the beginning, the aim was to create spirits for mixing in cocktails— "You shouldn't have to think hard about how to use them," according to Katz— and each release is wholly original. "Why make a spirit that tastes like something already out there?"

First to market was Perry's Tot Navy Strength gin, at 57% alcohol—a proof given the title "navy strength" by gin-swilling British sailors, the story goes, since it's sufficiently alcoholic that, if spilled on gunpowder, the gunpowder could still ignite. While the style of gin dated back hundreds of years, and played an important role in cocktail culture, "there hadn't been a navy-strength gin commercially available in the U.S. for nearly a century," according to Katz.

Dorothy Parker American gin followed, a contemporary gin with the unusual botanicals of elderberry and dried hibiscus. Next in line, Chief Gowanus New-Netherland gin, a recreation of the style that the Dutch would have distilled in Brooklyn when it was still a colony of the Netherlands: an unaged rye, redistilled with juniper and hops and barrel-aged for several months.

Ever historically minded, New York Distilling Co. then revived a whiskey style, once an American favorite but now little-known, known as Rock and Rye—rye whiskey with rock candy sugar and, in their recipe, Bing cherries, dried orange peel, and cinnamon bark. The result tastes something like a bottled Old Fashioned. "It's directly linked to the 19th-century saloon era; the spirit had significant popularity in its day." And most recently, the brand's Ragtime Rye: "We've been putting down barrels of rye whiskey since day one."

Housing a bar, The Shanty, within its distillery, New York Distilling has a home to showcase its spirits in cocktails as well as on their own. "We don't charge for tours," says Katz. "If you're already here and paying for a cocktail, it's the least we can do to invite you into our space, share that experience, and give you a tasting as well."

The following three cocktails showcase New York Distilling's products.

New York Distilling Co.

DOUBLE STANDARD SOUR
NATE DUMAS

¾ oz/20 mL Dorothy Parker American gin
¾ oz/20 mL Maker's Mark bourbon
1 oz/30 mL lemon juice
½ oz/15 mL grenadine (recipe p. 19)
¼ oz/10 mL simple syrup

Combine all the ingredients in a cocktail shaker with ice. Shake until well chilled and strain into a rocks glass over fresh ice. Garnish with an orange twist.

MARTINI ROBBINS
NATE DUMAS

1¼ oz/40 mL Mister Katz's Rock and Rye
1 oz/30 mL Dorothy Parker American gin
1 oz/30 mL Martini & Rossi sweet vermouth

Combine all the ingredients in a mixing glass with ice. Stir until well chilled and strain into a chilled coupe. Garnish with an orange twist.

UNSPEAKABLE-RESPECTABLE PUNCH (SERVES 10-12)
CREATED BY COCKTAIL HISTORIAN DAVID WONDRICH

1 750 mL bottle Chief Gowanus New-Netherland Gin
Peels of 4 lemons
½ cup sugar
1 cup lemon juice
4 oz/120 mL Luxardo maraschino
24 oz/675 mL chilled club soda

In a punch bowl, muddle the lemon peels with the sugar and let stand for 30 minutes. Add the fresh lemon juice and stir until the sugar has dissolved. Add the gin and maraschino and stir. Add 2 to 3 large blocks of ice and then add the club soda. Serve in punch glasses.

THE IMPROVED PENDENNIS CLUB COCKTAIL

Toby Cecchini, Long Island Bar

Gin, lime, and apricot: What's not to love? Toby Cecchini's version of this oft-overlooked classic uses both apricot liqueur and apricot eau-de-vie, with Peychaud's bitters contributing an elusive anise note.

2 oz/60 mL Plymouth gin
1 oz/30 mL fresh lime juice, strained
¾ oz/20 mL Giffard Abricot du Roussillon
½ oz/15 mL Purkhart Blume Marillen apricot
  eau-de-vie
¼ oz/10 mL rich simple syrup (2:1)
3 dashes Peychaud's bitters

Combine all the ingredients in a cocktail shaker with ice. Shake until well chilled and strain into a chilled coupe.

The Improved Pendennis Club Cocktail, Long Island Bar

700 SONGS GIMLET

Nate Dumas, The Shanty

"This will never go off the menu," says Allen Katz of this riff on the classic gimlet. "As a bar owner, you want people to keep drinking . . . within reason, of course. Here's a cocktail you can suck down with pleasure and order another right away."

1½ oz/45 mL Perry's Tot Navy Strength gin
¾ oz/20 mL lime juice
½ oz/15 mL simple syrup
¼ oz/10 mL cinnamon syrup (recipe p. 270)
4 dashes Bittermens Hellfire Shrub

Combine all the ingredients in a cocktail shaker with ice. Shake until well chilled and double-strain into a chilled coupe.

NINETY-NINE ROSES

Jonathan Kobritz, Hotel Delmano

One of Delmano's best-loved drinks, this drink is a perfect example of their sophisticated, straightforward style—a base of gin, ginger, and lemon with apricot and fragrant rose water playing on a higher register.

1½ oz/45 mL London dry gin
¾ oz/20 mL lemon juice
½ oz/15 mL apricot liqueur (Rothman &
  Winter Orchard recommended))
½ oz/15 mL ginger syrup (recipe p. 273)
Rose water

Combine all the ingredients except the rose water in a cocktail shaker with ice. Shake until well chilled and strain into a chilled coupe. Garnish with a lemon twist and 5 drops of rose water on the surface of the cocktail.

• WHO'S OLD TOM? •

When most of us think of gin, we imagine a spirit strong on the juniper and not at all sweet. Those are the characteristics of London dry gin—the predominant style, but not the only one. Old Tom gin first became popular in the 19th century, and many cocktail books of the era call for it by name.

Some Old Tom gins were sweetened, whereas others were not; some had a malty base, some were barrel-aged, others weren't. But unlike London dry gins, they could contain added sugar, and the juniper wasn't generally quite as predominant. "Old Tom gins can sometimes be used as a gateway for the novice gin-drinker," according to Joel Lee Kulp. "The flavors are often softer; it's still botanical, but has less of a huge juniper hit."

TOKYO FIR
GRAND FERRY TAVERN

The piney scent and flavor of Zirbenz picks up the juniper notes of the gin in this cocktail, with ginger adding a spice of its own. For ginger syrup, this bar uses a version made by P&H, a Brooklyn soda company.

1¾ oz/50 mL Ransom
Old Tom gin
½ oz/15 mL Zirbenz
Stone Pine liqueur
¼ oz/10 mL lemon juice
¼ oz/10 mL ginger syrup
¼ oz/10 mL sweet vermouth

Combine all the ingredients in a cocktail shaker with ice. Shake until well chilled and strain into a chilled coupe. Garnish with a lemon twist.

NORTH BY NORTHWEST
THE RICHARDSON

Floral-herbal Braulio amaro pairs well with Ransom's barrel-aged Old Tom gin, with lemon and orange liqueur to brighten it up.

1½ oz/45mL Ransom
Old Tom Gin
½ oz/15 mL lemon juice
½ oz/15 mL Braulio amaro
¼ oz/10 mL simple syrup
¼ oz/10 mL Combier
triple sec

Combine all the ingredients in a cocktail shaker with ice. Shake until well chilled and strain into a chilled coupe. Garnish with an orange twist.

MARTINEZ

A venerable cocktail that predates the Martini—indeed, the Martini is considered a descendant, and its name a derivative, of the Martinez—this classic is richer and gentler than its cousin, thanks to slightly sweet Old Tom gin, a heavy hand of vermouth, and the cherry liqueur Luxardo maraschino.

1½ oz/45 mL Hayman's
Old Tom Gin
1½ oz/45 mL Carpano
Antica Formula
sweet vermouth
1 tsp Luxardo maraschino
2 dashes Angostura bitters

Combine all the ingredients in a mixing glass with ice. Stir until well chilled and strain into a coupe. Garnish with a lemon twist.

BROOKLYN GIN

After more than ten years working in the spirits industry, Joe Santos and Emil Jattne shared the hope of opening a craft distillery—and a love for gin. "We started out with aspirations of making other spirits," says Santos, who founded the distillery together with Jattne in 2010, "but when we got going, we realized how intense it was, and we put everything else on hold!"

That focus has served them well, with Brooklyn Gin now selling nationally and internationally, and recently taking home several significant awards. While nearly all gins contain some citrus peels in their botanical blend, Brooklyn Gin distinguishes itself by using only fresh peels, not dried peels or extracted oils. "We love vibrant, aromatic gin that's heavy on citrus flavors," says Santos. "We're the only gin that uses 100% fresh citrus, from five different fruits. It gives the gin a real bright citrus note on the nose and palate."

Jattne and Santos are actively working to open a distillery in Brooklyn—they currently operate a pot still in Warwick, NY, a short trip outside the city—but from the beginning, have been involved in the Brooklyn bar world. "Brooklyn Gin is a great example of a brand that has real loyalty to this community," says Ian Hardie of Huckleberry Bar. "They're very engaged with the bars that they want to work with; they've been a big supporter of ours. It's really all about that mutual support."

But of course, bartenders gravitate toward products they're impressed with. "They produce a quality gin," says Hardie, "and they have a beautiful bottle. It helps that it looks really good on the back bar."

> **"We're the only gin that uses 100% fresh citrus, from five different fruits."**
> — *Joe Santos, Brooklyn Gin*

And it helps that their flavor profile is one that bartenders get excited to play with.

The following four cocktails are Brooklyn Gin favorites, showing off the gin's bright, citrus-forward style.

BEES KNEES

2 oz/60 mL Brooklyn gin
¾ oz/20 mL lemon juice
¾ oz/20 mL honey syrup (1:1)

Combine all the ingredients in a cocktail shaker with ice. Shake until well chilled and strain into a rocks glass filled with fresh ice. Garnish with a lemon wheel.

BROOKLYN G&T

2 oz Brooklyn Gin
4 oz Fever Tree tonic

Combine ingredients in a Collins glass over ice and stir gently. Garnish with a lime wheel, and/or slices of grapefruit, fresh rosemary, juniper berries, or black peppercorns.

DONT TAKE YOUR LOVE

Michael Neff, Holiday Cocktail Lounge

1½ oz/45 mL Brooklyn gin
1 oz/30 mL grapefruit juice
¼ oz/10 mL Fernet-Branca
Tonic water

Half-rim a highball glass with kosher salt. Fill with ice and add the gin, grapefruit juice, and Fernet. Stir to combine and fill with tonic. Garnish with a tall rosemary spear.

FOUNTAINHEAD

Damon Boelte, Grand Army

1 oz/30 mL Brooklyn gin
1 oz/30 mL oloroso sherry
¾ oz/20 mL lemon juice
¼ oz/10 mL Branca Menta
½ oz/15 mL simple syrup
Club soda

Combine the first five ingredients in a cocktail shaker with ice. Shake until well chilled and strain into a Collins glass filled with fresh ice. Top with club soda and garnish with a mint sprig and microplaned lemon zest.

BOX OF RAIN
Achilles Heel

An unusual rye-based, barrel-aged gin from New York Distilling Co. is at the heart of this lively cocktail perfumed with chamomile honey and topped with a dramatic float of red wine.

1½ oz/45 mL Chief Gowanus New-
    Netherland gin
¾ oz/20 mL chamomile honey (recipe p. 279)
¾ oz/20 mL Dolin blanc vermouth
¼ oz/10 mL lemon juice
½ oz/15 mL red wine (Syrah recommended)

Combine all the ingredients except the red wine in a cocktail shaker with ice. Shake until well chilled and strain into a coupe. Top with a float of red wine.

THE L.I.B. GIMLET
Toby Cecchini, Long Island Bar

Toby Cecchini calls himself a "super-classicist," though classics on his menu tend to have a distinctive twist—including this gimlet, made with a lime-ginger cordial that hits a perfect balance of tart, ginger-spicy, and sweet. The cordial itself is a several-day process, but keeps for weeks or more once made, and when it's on hand, this cocktail comes together in seconds.

2 oz/60 mL Tanqueray gin
1 oz/30 mL lime-ginger cordial (recipe p. 282)
¾ oz/20 mL fresh lime juice, strained

Combine all the ingredients in a cocktail shaker with ice and shake vigorously. Strain into a large rocks glass filled with cracked ice or, if preferred, a chilled cocktail coupe. Garnish with a thin wheel of lime floated atop.

Box of Rain, Achilles Heel

3 MORE GIN CLASSICS ...

AVIATION

One of those drinks that requires specialty ingredients—maraschino liqueur (which is quite versatile) and crème de violette (much less so)—but once you try this sophisticated cocktail, you'll have no problem getting through a bottle. Some versions eliminate the crème de violette; the resulting cocktail remains delicious but lacks the blue-purple hue and floral scent.

2 oz/60 mL gin
¾ oz/20 mL lemon juice
½ oz/15 mL maraschino liqueur
¼ oz/10 mL crème de violette

Combine all the ingredients in a cocktail shaker with ice. Shake until well chilled and strain into a coupe. Garnish with a brandied cherry.

RAMOS GIN FIZZ

An occasional joke in the industry: If you want to annoy a bartender, ask for a Ramos Gin Fizz. The amount of shaking required to properly whip up egg white and cream make this an extremely time-intensive cocktail (and hard on the forearms to boot). Don't be surprised if the bartender hands off the shaker halfway through to take a breather! That said, the Ramos is a true classic, silky and ethereally light when made properly, the orange flower water contributing a gentle, fragrant floral note.

2 oz/60 mL gin
½ oz/15 mL lemon juice
½ oz/15 mL lime juice
¾ oz/20 mL simple syrup
½ oz/15 mL cream
3 drops orange flower water
1 egg white
Club soda

Combine all the ingredients except the club soda in a cocktail shaker without ice. Shake vigorously for a "dry shake"—for at least a minute—then add ice and shake again, as long as you can stand to. Strain into a chilled Collins glass. Top with soda and garnish with an orange wedge.

THE REAL LAST WORD

An easy cocktail to riff on (see "Word," p. 174), the Last Word is a classic worth mastering, a precise balance of tart and herbaceous.

1 oz/30 mL gin
1 oz/30 mL green Chartreuse
1 oz/30 mL maraschino liqueur
1 oz/30 mL fresh lime juice

Combine all the ingredients in a cocktail shaker with ice. Shake until well chilled and strain into a coupe. Garnish with a brandied cherry.

The L.I.B. Gimlet, Long Island Bar

• ON THE •
G & T

CLASSIC G&T

Herbal gin and bittersweet tonic—probably the most versatile, complex, satisfying highball the world has ever known. With such a simple drink, details are key: Use plenty of ice, a high-quality tonic water, and a gin whose flavors you're partial to. You can't go wrong with a classic London dry like Beefeater or Tanqueray.

2 oz/60 mL London dry gin
4 oz/120 mL Fever Tree tonic

Combine the ingredients in a Collins glass over ice and stir gently. Garnish with a lime wedge.

FROZEN G&T
ROB KRUEGER, EXTRA FANCY

Think a gin and tonic is refreshing? A *frozen* gin and tonic has it beat. Extra Fancy had a hard time keeping enough tonic syrup in stock for this wildly popular blended drink. At the bar, they're using the tonic syrup that you'd purchase for a soda gun—essentially all the flavors of tonic, without the sparkling water—with some orange bitters dashed in for depth of flavor. Tonic syrup is available in stores too: Jack Rudy and Small Hand Foods both make great versions.

1½ oz/45 mL Hendricks gin
½ oz/15 mL tonic syrup
½ oz/15 mL simple syrup
¾ oz/20 mL lime juice

Combine all the ingredients in a blender with 1 cup of ice and blend until smooth. Pour into a glass and garnish with a lime wheel and a cucumber slice.

SPANISH-INSPIRED G&T

The British will always be thought of as the world's true gin drinkers, but the Spanish have adopted the gin and tonic—or "Gin Tonic"—as their national drink. Spanish G&Ts are served in huge balloon glasses and go crazy with the garnishes, understanding that different herbs, spices, and citrus will pair differently with any given gin. Here, grapefruit rind and coriander pick up on several of the botanicals in Beefeater 24.

2 oz/60 mL Beefeater 24 gin
4 oz/120 mL Fever Tree tonic

Combine the ingredients in a large balloon glass with several ice cubes. Garnish with two grapefruit twists and a pinch of whole coriander seeds.

CITRUS MEDICA
KATE O'CONNOR MORRIS, ROSE'S

Try to get your hands on a bottle of this cult-favorite gin from Menorca. It's a well-chosen base for this dressed-up Spanish Gin Tonic, huge on the citrus peels and with the unexpected addition of yuzu juice, a sour Japanese citrus fruit.

2 oz/60 mL Mahon Xoriguer gin
¾ oz/20 mL yuzu juice
3 dashes Regan's orange bitters
Tonic water (Fever Tree recommended)
6 to 8 lemon, lime, and orange peels

Place two citrus peels in the bottom of a Collins glass. Add the yuzu, gin, and several ice cubes. Add two more citrus peels and the orange bitters. Top with tonic and the remaining citrus peels.

EXTRA FANCY

CHAPTER 3

VODKA

Ask today's Brooklyn bartenders about vodka, and you'll get a web of conflicting answers. On the one hand, vodka is a chameleon, able to pair with almost any flavor—and a vodka drink is often the best-selling one on a cocktail list. On the other hand, vodka is still associated with the featureless, liqueur-laden drinks of past decades, and bartenders aren't often fans.

In a way, this makes sense. Gin, whiskey, rum, tequila—any of these spirits has distinct and obvious character, whether from the plants they're distilled from (agave, grapes, rye), the way they're flavored (gin botanicals), or the way they're aged (any brown liquor). Bartenders appreciate spirits with layers of nuance and flavor that they can play up or play with.

As an unflavored, unaged spirit, vodka is flavorless by design. And in a way, that's why it's so popular; those who don't like other cocktails often do like vodka. To bartenders, it's not a particularly challenging spirit, and therefore not an interesting one; some craft cocktail bars don't have a single vodka drink on the menu, and others will go even further, not carrying the spirit at all.

Yet vodka drinks will always have their devotees, and vodka is endlessly versatile; it's hard to find flavors that can't pair with it. And many bartenders have shifted from a mentality of "We only serve cocktails that we like" to "Give the customer what they want." Vodka-sodas are a bartender shorthand for "booze, no flavor"—but so what? "When people object to making vodka-sodas, I think that's silly and mean," says Meaghan Montagano of Extra Fancy in Williamsburg. "Even if you'd rather make more elaborate cocktails, alcohol is the gateway to more alcohol. If you refuse them, there's no booze to soften them up!"

"There's no spirit that I'm afraid of," says Robert Krueger, also of Extra Fancy. "There's no bar-shaming here—that happens way too often in cocktail bars. That's not what we want to do."

EXTRA FANCY

It's safe to say that any bar—at least, any bar that's doing its job—wants its patrons to have a good time. But I've never found a bar that tries quite as hard to deliver as Extra Fancy in Williamsburg. One part seafood restaurant, one part industry hangout, Fancy is an unqualified good time, from the disco ball on the ceiling to the always-popular frozen cocktails. Muscle shirts and trucker hats come emblazoned with their logo. Cocktail names are all presented with a wink—from the rum-Aperol-melon Rum Cougar Meloncamp to the Ultimate Hipster Girlfriend, perhaps the highest ironic praise a Williamsburg bar could bestow: rosé and a shot of Evan Williams.

But amidst all the merriment lurks a truly sophisticated cocktail bar, where even drinks called Honey, I Spiced the Kids and Frozemonade (or Frozemonade®, as they'd hoped to call it) display a level of sophistication and mixology acumen. "It's a low-key place with high standards," says co-owner and bar director Rob Krueger. A five-year veteran of seminal Manhattan cocktail bar Employees Only, Krueger and team can talk esoteric spirits with the best of them—but are just as happy making vodka drinks or pouring bourbon shots. "Cocktails should be fun and drinkable," says Krueger. The drink you want to reorder, and then maybe have two more. "Our new favorite hashtag is #chuggability."

Everything about Extra Fancy seems to have a backstory—even its origins. "I'd moved into a new apartment that had a little back patio, so I went on Craigslist to look for a patio table," says co-owner Mark Rancourt. "And when I searched, a restaurant *with* a patio popped up. They weren't selling the patio tables, but the whole patio. And the restaurant attached to it." It was a true find, with a highly trafficked location on Metropolitan Avenue, the neighborhood of Williamsburg evolving around it, and a generous patio that opened the space up considerably.

Mention Extra Fancy to New York bartenders, and you're likely to find more than a few regulars. "We wanted to be a home for people in the restaurant business," says Krueger—open until 4 a.m. every night of the week to accommodate late-night schedules; fun, unpretentious, genuine.

"And though it's a bar for industry, it's just as much a bar for our neighbors," says general manager Meaghan Montagano, who was herself a neighborhood regular before joining the Extra Fancy team. "We talk to them, embrace them, let them join in on the party. And I think you can feel that when you walk in." Krueger concurs. "It's a fun and relaxed place where people can be themselves—both the people who work here, and the people who come in through the door."

> **" It's a fun and relaxed place where people can be themselves— both people who work here and the people who come in through the door. "**
> — *Meaghan Montagano, Extra Fancy*

COCKTAIL RECIPES

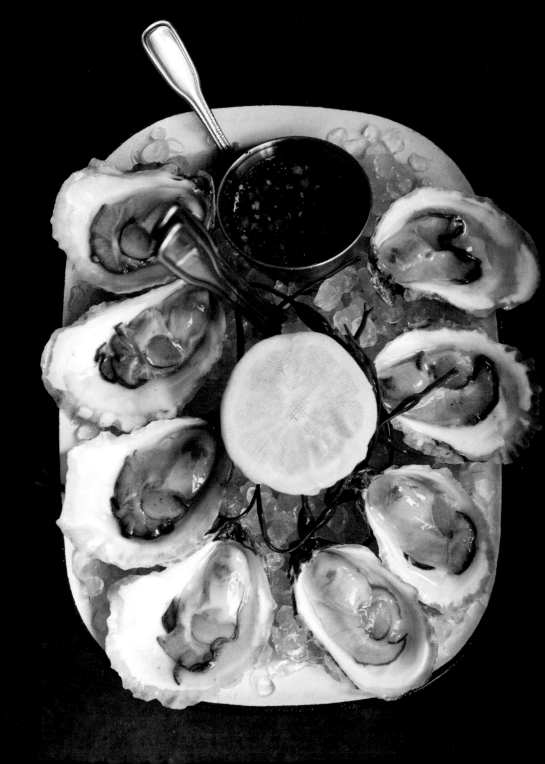

"Cocktails should be fun and drinkable … the drink you want to reorder, and then maybe have two more."

— Rob Krueger, Extra Fancy

Baby, You're Driving, Extra Fancy

BABY, YOU'RE DRIVING

Rob Krueger, Extra Fancy

When the team at Extra Fancy was testing out cocktails before the bar first opened, co-owner Mark Rancourt's girlfriend took one sip of this cocktail, handed him the car keys, and said, "Baby, you're driving." (Quite an endorsement.) Zubrowka is a traditional Polish vodka flavored with bison grass, for a complex spirit that's faintly grassy-woodsy, has a strong vanilla note, and works exceptionally well in cocktails.

1 oz/30 mL Zubrowka Bison Grass vodka
1 oz/30 mL Lillet Blanc
1 oz/30 mL Combier pamplemousse rose
1 oz/30 mL lime juice

Combine all the ingredients in a cocktail shaker with ice. Shake until well chilled and double-strain into a coupe. Garnish with a grapefruit peel cut into the shape of a star, and a mint sprig.

O.V.C.

Jay Zimmerman, Ba'sik

Chamomile, honey, and lemon give this shaken drink a familiar, friendly character, stiffened up with vodka and balanced by Angostura bitters.

2 oz/60 mL Aylesbury Duck vodka
¾ oz/20 mL chamomile honey syrup
(recipe p. 279)
¾ oz/20 mL lemon juice
3 dashes Angostura bitters

Combine all the ingredients in a cocktail shaker with ice. Shake until well chilled and strain into a chilled coupe. Garnish with a lemon wedge.

STONE OF JORDAN

Tom Dixon, Roberta's

Flavored vodkas were all the rage ten years ago, but virtually every bartender will prefer to flavor their own vodka, which, incidentally, couldn't be simpler. And once you have a bottle of cucumber–pink peppercorn vodka, this shaken drink comes together in minutes.

2 oz/60 mL cucumber and pink peppercorn–
infused vodka (recipe p. 264)
¾ oz/20 mL lime juice
½ oz/15 mL crème de cassis
½ oz/15 mL simple syrup

Combine all the ingredients in a cocktail shaker with ice. Shake until well chilled and double-strain into a coupe.

WHAT DEFINES A
SUCCESSFUL COCKTAIL?

Why do some cocktails become classics, and why do some modern cocktails really take off, gaining respect (and often imitation) in the bar community? In both cases, there's a certain unity to the drink—one central idea being conveyed, a powerful totality rather than competing parts. And in both cases, understanding the drink is intuitive, even if you've never come across it before.

"Drinks should be conceptualized very easily; the sense of *'This is what this drink is'* should be immediately apparent," says Rob Krueger of Extra Fancy. "It should have a purpose and an audience." His "Frozemonade"—a frozen rose lemonade, is a perfect example; Krueger also cites the Penicillin, a Scotch sour with honey-ginger syrup created by New York bartender Sam Ross.

"I call them 'Girl Jumping Out of a Cake' drinks," says St. John Frizell of Fort Defiance. "Have you ever seen a girl jumping out of a cake? Probably not, right? But you know exactly what I'm talking about regardless. You don't have to think about what that means, or what the occasion is. That's what an Irish Coffee is to me. Most people have never had one, or have never had a *real* one, and yet they intuitively grasp what it is."

> ❝ It's always about making these harmonious little masterpieces, and that's such a cool thing to be part of. ❞
>
> —Del Pedro, Tooker Alley

With his musical background, Del Pedro of Tooker Alley brings a different perspective. "In a way, we're all creating pop songs," he says. "A cocktail is this discrete little thing, like a three-minute pop song; it's so quick and disposable, but you want to make it a little masterpiece. Whatever angle we're coming at cocktails from, it's always about making these harmonious little masterpieces, and that's such a cool thing to be part of."

Frozemonade, Extra Fancy

GREENWOOD COOLER

David Moo, Quarter Bar

Named for the cemetery next to the bar, this cooler is Quarter Bar's signature summer drink; who's immune to the charms of grapefruit, mint, and cucumber?

1¾ oz/50 mL Luksusowa vodka
¾ oz/20 mL grapefruit juice
¼ oz/10 mL simple syrup
3 mint leaves
2 thin cucumber wheels
1 lemon wedge
Club soda

Muddle one cucumber slice, the mint leaves, and the lemon wedge in the bottom of a highball glass. Add the vodka, grapefruit juice, simple syrup, and ice. Pour the drink into a shaking tin and back into the glass several times. Fill with club soda. Garnish with the remaining cucumber wheel.

PARKS & LEISURE

Blueprint

Orange-rhubarb Aperol and grapefruit juice are two ingredients that just work together; the addition of vodka and lime to this cocktail from popular Park Slope bar Blueprint make this a simple and very drinkable cocktail.

1½ oz/45 mL Wodka vodka
1 oz/30 mL grapefruit juice
½ oz/15 mL Aperol
½ oz/15 mL lime juice
¼ oz/10 mL simple syrup

Combine all the ingredients in a cocktail shaker with ice. Shake until well chilled and strain into a Collins glass with crushed ice. Garnish with a grapefruit twist.

Greenwood Cooler, Quarter Bar

BROOKLYN MULE

John Bush, Pork Slope

So simple but so compelling, the vodka lime-ginger Moscow Mule is an enduring classic. John Bush's version is slightly tweaked, with Pickett's spicy ginger beer and a bit of simple syrup to balance its intensity.

1½ oz/45 mL Brooklyn Republic vodka
½ oz/15 mL lime juice
½ oz/15 mL simple syrup
4 to 5 oz/150 to 180 mL Pickett's spicy
    ginger beer

In a highball glass with ice, combine the first three ingredients. Fill with ginger beer. Garnish with a lime wedge.

CLASSIC MOSCOW MULE

Vodka, lime, and ginger beer—it's both a reliably awesome drink and a fun format to experiment with. Those who want a mellow ginger flavor can use a milder ginger beer, but ginger addicts can go as high-powered as they want.

2 ounces vodka
½ oz lime juice
4–5 ounces ginger beer

In a Moscow Mule mug, or a highball glass with ice, combine vodka and lime. Fill with ginger beer. Garnish with a lime wedge.

ONE IN A MELON
Meaghan Montagano, Extra Fancy

Though they're in the minority, there are high-quality flavored vodkas out there; Crop Cucumber Organic is one example. Watermelon, cucumber, and melon make this cocktail an incredibly appealing summer drink.

1½ oz/45 mL Crop Cucumber Organic vodka
2½ oz/75 mL fresh watermelon water
  (watermelon blended into juice,
  then strained)
1 oz/30 mL Carpano bianco vermouth
¾ oz/20 mL lemon juice
¼ oz/10 mL Luxardo maraschino liqueur
2 dashes Peychaud's bitters

Combine all the ingredients in a cocktail shaker with ice. Shake until well chilled and strain into a Collins glass with fresh ice. Garnish with a horse's neck lemon twist, which is a long, thin lemon peel spiral.

EGYPTIAN SPRING
Nathan Ricke, Esme

Some spirits are so aggressive as to overwhelm almost any other flavor, like the anise powerhouse *arak* from the Middle East (similar to Turkish *raki* or Greek *ouzo*). That's where vodka comes in, taming the anise so it's a suitable match for these distinctly Mediterranean flavors. Greek yogurt seems surprising, but it gives the cocktail a silky, slightly creamy texture that works perfectly.

1 oz/30 mL vodka
1 oz/30 mL arak (ouzo can substitute)
¾ oz/20 mL lemon juice
½ oz/15 mL rich honey syrup (2:1 honey
  to water)
1 tsp Greek yogurt
Pinch of kosher salt

Combine all the ingredients in a cocktail shaker with ice. Shake until well chilled and strain into a Collins glass with fresh ice. Garnish with a thin lemon wheel.

VESPER

Invented by James Bond (or rather, his author) in *Casino Royale*, the Vesper bridges the gulf between gin and vodka drinkers. "It's a more interesting, citrusy take on a Martini and a good introduction for vodka drinkers to drink gin!" says Tonia Guffey of Dram.

2 oz/60 mL gin
1 oz/30 mL vodka
1 oz/30 mL Lillet or Cocchi Americano

Combine all the ingredients in a mixing glass with several cracked ice cubes. Stir until well chilled and strain into a chilled coupe. Garnish with a lemon twist.

East Ender, Roberta's

EAST ENDER

Tom Dixon, Roberta's

Homemade flavored vodkas can be
sophisticated, or they can just be *fun*—like
this maraschino cherry vodka, designed for
Roberta's often-rowdy, always-lively outdoor
bar. It might not make it onto the menu of a
craft cocktail bar, but bring this to a party and
it's guaranteed to disappear.

3 oz/90 mL maraschino cherry vodka
  (recipe p. 269)
4 oz/120 mL lemonade (or combine 1 oz/
  30 mL lemon juice, ½ oz/15 mL simple
  syrup, and 2½ oz/75 mL water)

Fill a pint glass with ice and pour in the
lemonade, then the cherry vodka. Garnish
with a lemon wheel.

PORCH SWING COLLINS

Jen Marshall, Butter & Scotch

The lemongrass comes through beautifully in
this cocktail designed by Jen Marshall: "It
plays to my style of mixing savory flavors, like
aromatic lemongrass, with the typical sweet
flavors you usually find in a cocktail," she says.

1½ oz/45 mL lemongrass-infused Reyka
  vodka (recipe p. 264)
¾ oz/20 mL lemon juice
¾ oz/20 mL simple syrup
½ oz/15 mL fresh cucumber juice
Club soda

Combine all the ingredients except the soda
in a cocktail shaker with ice. Shake until well
chilled and strain into a Collins glass filled
with fresh ice. Fill with club soda. Garnish
with a cucumber wheel and a straw.

CHILI LIME

Quarter Bar

We've seen vodka pair with sweet flavors,
savory, herbal—so why not spicy? A blazing
hot sauce from Trinidad & Tobago lights up
this cocktail, along with serrano chile, their
combined heat reined in just a bit with Sprite.
"This was invented by my friend Rahul
Chakravartty and his cousins while they were
stuck in a hotel during a monsoon somewhere in India," says Quarter Bar's David
Moo. Unpredictable but awesome.

1¾ oz/50 mL vodka
½ serrano chile, split lengthwise
½ oz/15 mL lime juice
1 nickel-sized amount of Matouk's
  Flambeau hot sauce
Sprite
Club soda

Combine the first four ingredients in a
highball glass with ice and stir together.
Fill with 2 parts Sprite to 1 part club soda.

QUARTER BAR

A New York bartender for nearly two decades, David Moo developed an interest in cocktails well before most bars or restaurants had anything approaching a sophisticated cocktail program. But by the early 2000s, he'd started to find other like-minded individuals. "I was a regular at a bar called Barramundi, one of my beloved places," he says—right down the street from foundational Manhattan cocktail bar Milk and Honey. "We were some of the first regulars," says Moo. "We'd make CDs for Sasha" (owner Sasha Petraske); "He'd pick our brains about music and we'd pick his brain about cocktails." Petraske had insights that, at the time, seemed surprising—as simple as, "I go into old book shops looking for cocktail books." Inasmuch as there was a cocktail scene, Moo found his way into it. "That was the beginning of me being truly interested in cocktails. I'd pick the brains of cocktail bartenders whenever I could, although back then, there were about seven of them."

Over the years, Moo fell deeper into the cocktail world, as head bartender at acclaimed restaurant Ouest, where he had access to the resources of a full kitchen; and at a well-loved "neighborhood arty dive" in Brooklyn called Last Exit. "One day, I was talking to one of the owners, nattering on about high-end bitters or something like that—and this guy is not a cocktail geek, he's an Irish carpenter who owned a few bars." That owner had just signed a lease on a new space farther south in Brooklyn.

That was the origin of Quarter Bar, which opened in 2007; in the southern reaches of Park Slope, it's set apart from Brooklyn's well-trafficked nightlife corridors, but has all the more loyal following for it. "We call ourselves a neighborhood cocktail bar—and both those halves are important," says Moo. "We made decisions early on, that although we were going to make fine cocktails here, we wouldn't make them super precious. We don't want to alienate the person who just wants to come in and drink their High Life." And the cocktails themselves are similarly inviting, whether the grapefruit-mint-cucumber Greenwood Cooler in warmer months, or the Old Fashioned–like Two Bits in the winter. Quarter Bar can make you believe that every neighborhood local could serve incredible cocktails; and, simultaneously, every cocktail bar could have all the character of a neighborhood local.

COCKTAIL RECIPES

Alice's Mallet (p. 41)
Two Bits (p. 95)
Greenwood Cooler (p. 68)
Chili Lime (p. 71)
King's Town Punch (p. 130)
Sea Shandy (p. 250)
Rosarita (p. 156)

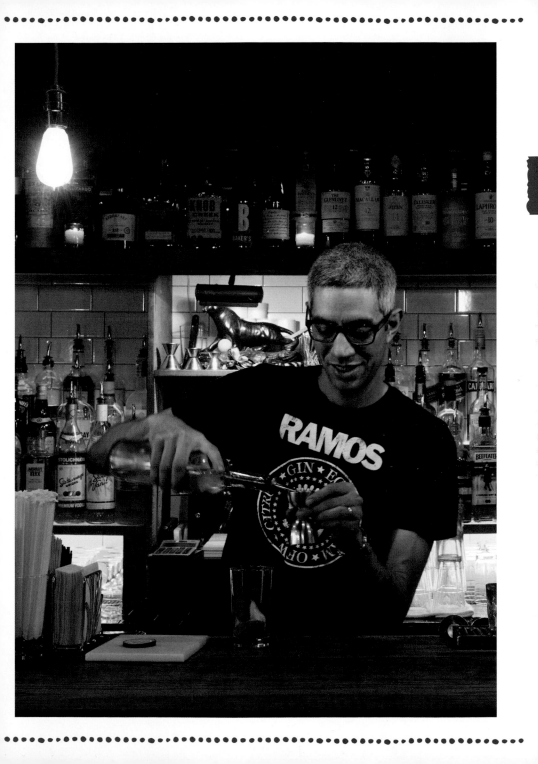

" We call ourselves a neighborhood cocktail bar—and both those halves are important. "

—David Moo, Quarter Bar

THE COMPLICATED HISTORY
OF THE COSMOPOLITAN

Few drinks have had as rapid an ascent—and such a quick backlash—as the Cosmopolitan. (Or if you're on familiar terms, the Cosmo.) While others claim to have played a part in the drink's invention, Toby Cecchini of Long Island Bar first created the Cosmopolitan as we know it, while bartending at The Odeon in Tribeca in 1988.

Friends had told him about a drink served in "gnarly leather bars in San Francisco," in Cecchini's words, called the Cosmopolitan: vodka, Rose's grenadine, and Rose's lime juice. The name and the color appealed, "but the drink itself was ghastly," he says. So he developed an alternative: Absolut Citron vodka, which had just come on the market, orange liqueur, fresh lime, and cranberry for that vibrant red.

Cecchini first made the drink for The Odeon's waitresses, "since I wanted to get on their good side." It caught on, and not just amongst the staff: Waitresses recommended the Cosmopolitan to customers, who started ordering it; others saw the eye-catching cocktail and called for a round; regulars soon asked for the drink by name—and at the time, the Odeon counted Madonna and Sandra Bernhard among its regulars. The drink, to Cecchini's amazement, caught on across Tribeca, New York, and, eventually, the globe.

In the craft cocktail world, the Cosmo is often held up as a poster child for the much-maligned, brightly colored drinks of its era—the order of unadventurous drinkers, camouflaging a spirit rather than highlighting it; the epitome of trend-driven drinking, popularized by *Sex and the City* and its ilk. Ubiquitous as it became, it was inevitable that bad Cosmos proliferated—with inferior triple sec, or lime juice that wasn't fresh, or any other of hundreds of possible minor sins against cocktails.

But in its original form, the Cosmopolitan is essentially a sour—spirit, citrus, orange liqueur—in the same family of drinks as a sidecar or a margarita. And as one of the only drinks of recent decades to become an enduring classic, its influence can't be disputed. "It sounds silly now, but before the Cosmopolitan, it never occurred to me that you *could* invent new cocktails," says Del Pedro of Tooker Alley, who bartended in Manhattan at the time. "To see someone creating a contemporary drink, rather than just making the classics—it was eye-opening."

> **" It sounds silly now, but before the Cosmopolitan, it never occurred to me that you could invent new cocktails. "**
>
> —Del Pedro, Tooker Alley

Whatever your feelings on the Cosmo, judge it on its true merits, with Cecchini's original specs.

TOBY CECCHINI'S COSMOPOLITAN

2 oz/60 mL Absolut Citron vodka
1 oz/30 mL Cointreau
1 oz/30 mL fresh lime juice, strained
1 oz/30 mL Ocean Spray cranberry juice cocktail

Combine all ingredients in a cocktail shaker with ice. Shake until well chilled and strain into a chilled cocktail coupe. Garnish with a lemon twist.

Grand Army

LIKE IT WITH VODKA? TRY IT WITH GIN

As many a bartender will tell you, gin is, essentially, a flavored vodka; flavored with juniper and other botanicals, that is. So many drinks with vodka adapt quite well to gin, and vice versa. Here are three classic cocktails that are just as clean, crisp, and refreshing—and a little more complex—when you try them with gin. Either way, you'll have an excellent drink.

SOUTHSIDE

2 oz/60 mL gin or vodka
1 oz/30 mL lime juice
½ oz/15 mL simple syrup
5 mint leaves

Combine all the ingredients in a cocktail shaker with ice. Shake until well chilled and double-strain into a chilled coupe. Garnish with a mint leaf.

TOM COLLINS

2 oz/60 mL gin or vodka
1 oz/30 mL lemon juice
¾ oz/20 mL simple syrup
2 oz/60 mL club soda

Combine the first three ingredients in a cocktail shaker with ice. Shake until well chilled and strain into a Collins glass with fresh ice. Top with soda. Garnish with a lemon wheel.

CLASSIC GIMLET

2 oz/60 mL gin or vodka
1 oz/30 mL lime juice
½ oz/15 mL simple syrup

Combine all the ingredients in a cocktail shaker with ice. Shake until well chilled and strain into a coupe or a rocks glass with fresh ice. Garnish with a lime wheel.

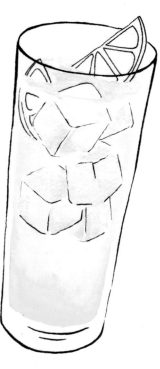

PORK SLOPE

What do three successful restaurant owners do when their neighborhood doesn't have a great after-hours bar? Open their own.

Dale Talde, David Massoni, and John Bush all appreciated the fun and energy of a great dive bar; after endless hours at their restaurants Talde and Thistle Hill Tavern, the last thing they wanted was a stuffy cocktail temple . . . more like a cold beer and a shot of bourbon. So their Pork Slope—in the neighborhood of Park Slope, thus the name—has a low-key, lived-in energy; not quite a dive, but with the welcoming, come-as-you-are vibe of the best dive bars.

Brooklyn bars come in many guises; Pork Slope, unlike most of the bars in this book, is the sort of place you can inhale a cheeseburger while watching college football. But it's also the sort of place you can taste your way through Maryland ryes or lesser-known Kentucky bourbons with a knowledgeable bartender as your guide. A beer and whiskey bar in spirit, Pork Slope has extensive selections of each, and a rotating shot-and-beer "Slippery Slope" inexpensive enough to justify its name.

But John Bush's cocktail list is strong in its own way—similarly accessible, whether tongue-in-cheek such as the rose-Aperol Redneck Hot Tub (suggested as a "food pairing": Cheez Doodles) or classic whiskey drinks such as the Boulevardier riff Capone's Cocktail. (And if you just want a Miller High Life and a basket of fries, Pork Slope's got you there, too.)

"I'm a whiskey guy at heart," says Bush. "I like Manhattans and Old Fashioneds and any kind of play on those. Instead of tricking out my back bar with all these different bottles to make one cocktail, I thought, why not just go all-in on whiskey—put together the best whiskey selection I can get my hands on, and see if people appreciate it?

"Our inspiration was honky-tonk, rock and roll, Roadhouse—it really was what we wanted, when we got off work, the bar we wanted to head to at midnight. The kind of place we could really love, and hopefully the neighborhood would love and embrace it, too. And to a big extent, they have."

COCKTAIL RECIPES

Redneck Hot Tub (p. 253)
Brooklyn Mule (p. 68)
Capone's Cocktail (p. 218)
Strong Island Shandy (p. 250)

1 BLOODY MARY MIX, 5 WAYS

The Bloody Mary is an outlier in the drinking world—it's savory where other cocktails are sweet; it's "acceptable" to drink in the morning, whereas other cocktails are not. And yet it's impossible to resist—or resist playing with. A classic Bloody, just spicy enough, is a beautiful thing; but it's also a template for experimentation. (That it's a guaranteed next-morning antidote to overimbibing any of these cocktails is just a bonus.)

BLOODY MARY MIX

This Bloody Mary base may have a number of ingredients, but once made, making any Bloody variant is as easy as adding booze and serving. (It's delicious sans alcohol, too.) It's essential to make this at least 12 hours before drinking so all the flavors can properly integrate. When refrigerated, the mix will last at least a week.

23 oz/700 mL tomato juice
6 Tbsp prepared horseradish
2 Tbsp Worcestershire sauce
1 oz/30 mL lemon juice
1 oz/30 mL olive brine
6 big dashes Tabasco
1 tsp salt
1 tsp celery salt
1 tsp coarse-ground black pepper
1/2 tsp celery seed

In a quart-sized container, combine all the ingredients and stir thoroughly. Cover and refrigerate overnight for the flavors to properly combine. Taste and season with additional salt, pepper, or Tabasco as desired.

CLASSIC BLOODY MARY

4 oz/120 mL Bloody Mary mix (p. 84)
1½ oz/45 mL vodka

In a Collins glass with ice, stir together the Bloody Mary mix and vodka. Garnish with a celery stalk, lemon wheel, and one or two olives.

BLOODY MARIA

Tequila is a match for anything spiced, so unaged tequila makes a perfect Bloody. Add a spicy garnish like a pickled jalapeño.

4 oz/120 mL Bloody Mary mix (p. 84)
1½ oz/45 mL blanco tequila

In a Collins glass with ice, stir together the Bloody Mary mix and tequila. Garnish with a lime wedge and a pickled jalapeño pepper.

RYE BLOODY MARY

Spicy in a different sort of way, high-proof rye is a better match for this Bloody than bourbon. As for the garnish, bacon and whiskey are always a good idea.

4 oz/120 mL Bloody Mary mix (p. 84)
1½ oz/45 mL Rittenhouse rye

In a Collins glass with ice, stir together the Bloody Mary mix and rye. Garnish with a celery stalk and a piece of bacon.

RED SNAPPER

While an unflavored spirit like vodka plays up the spice in the Bloody mix, gin brings out its characteristic herbaceousness.

4 oz/120 mL Bloody Mary mix (p. 84)
1½ oz/45 mL gin

In a Collins glass with ice, stir together the Bloody Mary mix and gin. Garnish with a celery stalk and several gherkins and olives on a skewer.

MEZCAL MARY

Tequila's cousin mezcal adds a powerful, smoky backdrop, making for an incredible Bloody.

4 oz/120 mL Bloody Mary mix (p. 84)
1½ oz/45 mL mezcal
Cayenne salt (3 Tbsp salt mixed with 1 tsp cayenne pepper)

In a Collins glass rimmed with cayenne salt and filled with ice, stir together the Bloody Mary mix and mezcal. Garnish with a lime wheel.

THE NARROWS

WHISKEY

W e've already laid out the ten essential bottles every would bo bartender should have. But if you were to strip it down to two, here's what I'd recommend: a bottle of gin, and a bottle of whiskey. (My own default would be rye, but bourbon drinkers, I'll give you that, too.)

Whiskey is versatile. It figures in many of our most important classics, from the Manhattan and the Old Fashioned on down. Two key whiskeys are proudly American: Rye and bourbon have a rich history in the States. And what can I say—it's delicious; unlike gin, it's as easy to sip straight as it is when embedded in a cocktail.

To talk about whiskey, it's important to start with a definition. Whiskey is a spirit made from a mash of grains—corn, rye, wheat, and malted barley all play various roles in various whiskeys. The composition of grains (say, 60% corn, 12% barley, and so on) is known as the "mashbill." The mash is cooked, fermented, then distilled. What most of us think of as "whiskey" is then aged in barrels. (Unaged white whiskey is a whole different animal. We'll get to that later.)

The vast majority of American whiskeys can be classified as bourbon or rye. In general—though every brand does differ—bourbon, which must be predominantly made from corn, is on the mellower, sweeter side; rye, drier and spicier. (Just think of the difference between cornbread and rye bread, and you'll get an idea.)

While brown spirits fell out of fashion at the end of the 20th century, when vodka was the bar-goer's drink of choice, they're back with a vengeance—so popular that some distillers are experiencing a shortage. (After all, aged spirits can't age overnight.) Ask bartenders about their favorite whiskey cocktails and you'll find yourself overwhelmed with the possibilities.

THE NARROWS

"Well-made cocktails and truly friendly people—that's what we've always aimed for," says Keith Kenji Cochran, co-owner of The Narrows in Bushwick. First opened in 2010, the bar was a pioneer both on its stretch of barren Flushing Avenue and in Bushwick as a whole. "It was such a local bar, at first," says manager Liz Stauber. "People were so happy to have *somewhere* to go. It had ambience, it was classy, it was comfortable—and a little bit special, because you had to be in the know to be there."

"Five years ago, no one was coming to Bushwick for a Friday night out. No one thought you could get well-made cocktails in Bushwick. But today, we get people coming in from all over Brooklyn, and Manhattan too."

"We try to keep things streamlined, and make the ingredients shine. It's the way we like to drink cocktails. "

—Liz Stauber, The Narrows

The clean, sparse look of The Narrows's bar reflects their philosophy toward both ambience and cocktails: According to Cochran, "We have a minimalist approach, in our design as well as our menu." Stauber concurs. "A lot of ingredients doesn't necessarily mean a drink is better, or has more flavor—or even that it's more interesting," she says. "We try to keep things streamlined, and make the ingredients shine. It's the way *we* like to drink cocktails."

It's an approach reflected in Caulfield's Dream, an eminently drinkable cocktail of bourbon, mint, lemon, and a float of sparkling cava; and the Pilar, its mezcal lightened with the aperitifs Cappelletti and Cocchi Americano.

Open until 4 a.m. every night of the week, The Narrows has always attracted an after-work industry crowd—particularly in its early days, when Bushwick was short on drinking options. "We'd get everyone from a fancy executive chef, to a bar back working around the corner, and everyone in between," says Cochran. Once they shut the doors for the night, the party would continue at Tina's, a "trucker diner" across the street that opened at 3:30 a.m. "There was a real sense of being in this special community."

These days, The Narrows counts cocktail drinkers from across the city among its fans, lured by its low-key charm and, especially in the summer, its lush back garden scrupulously maintained by co-owner Matt Webber's mother, Andrea. But neighborhood regulars are still the core of its business. "One of our regulars told me, 'I love coming here because I know exactly what it's going to be,' and I love that," says Stauber. "We strive for a consistent vibe—so even if you've never met one of the bartenders, he'll be friendly, he'll introduce himself to you, and he'll make you a great drink.

"Those things were initially so important to us—and they still are today."

COCKTAIL RECIPES

❝ Five years ago, no one was coming to Bushwick for a Friday night out. No one thought you could get well-made cocktails in Bushwick. But today, we get people coming in from all over Brooklyn, and Manhattan too. ❞

—Liz Stauber, The Narrows

KNOW YOUR
WHISKEYS

BOURBON

Contrary to much popular lore, bourbon does not have to be distilled in Kentucky (though 95% of it is). It does have to be distilled in America to be labeled as "bourbon," from a mashbill of at least 51% corn, and aged in charred new American oak barrels. A great entry point for those getting to know brown spirits.

RYE

American ryes follow similar guidelines: at least 51% rye in the mashbill, aged in charred new oak. (Canada is the other major rye producer.)

TENNESSEE WHISKEY

Jack Daniel's, made in Lynchburg, Tennessee, is far and away the best known. Similar to bourbon, but undergoes an additional step of charcoal mellowing.

SCOTCH

Made only in Scotland, naturally enough, from a mashbill of primarily or entirely malted barley, aged in oak barrels. "Single malt" whisky is made from only malted barley, at a single distillery. Blended Scotch whisky can draw from multiple distilleries and can include grain whisky, made from grains other than malted barley, in that blend.

IRISH WHISKEY

Generally lighter in body than Scotch whisky. Many higher-end Irish whiskeys are triple-distilled in a pot still, while most blends are a mix of pot still whiskey and grain whiskey.

AND ALL THE REST

While America, Scotland, Canada, and Ireland together provide most of the world's whiskey, other countries produce their own; Japan's single malt–style whiskys are of particular note.

BOURBON

POPPA'S PRIDE
Jay Zimmerman, Ba'sik

This cocktail—which Ba'sik owner Jay Zimmerman invented for Arcade Fire's frontman Win Butler, at the band's New York afterparty—got its name when Butler requested "a drink that my grandfather would be proud of." It's been on Ba'sik's menu since the bar's opening.

2 oz/60 mL bourbon
1 oz/30 mL ginger syrup (recipe p. 273)
5 mint leaves
2 lemon wedges
Club soda

Combine all the ingredients except the soda in a cocktail shaker with ice. Shake until well chilled, strain into a rocks glass over fresh ice, and top with soda. Float large dashes of Angostura bitters over the top.

Poppa's Pride, Ba'sik

BROOKLYN EAGLE
John Bush, Thistle Hill Tavern

John Bush starts from the whiskey-vermouth Manhattan template, then turns it into a shaken drink with orange liqueur and lime.

2 oz/60 mL Maker's Mark bourbon
1 oz/30 mL Carpano Antica Formula
  sweet vermouth
½ oz/15 mL orange liqueur
½ oz/15 mL lime juice

Combine all the ingredients in a cocktail shaker with ice. Shake until well chilled and strain into a rocks glass over fresh ice. Garnish with three cherries.

THE BIG RED ONE
Grand Ferry Tavern

At Grand Ferry Tavern, The Big Red One is so popular, they've put it on tap. Rather than bitters, there's a healthy pour of intensely herbal-bitter Fernet-Branca, the obsession of many a bartender.

2 oz/60 mL Wild Turkey 101 bourbon
¾ oz/20 mL Fernet-Branca
¼ oz/10 mL simple syrup

Combine all the ingredients in a mixing glass with ice. Stir until well chilled and strain into a double rocks glass with fresh ice.

CLASSIC WHISKEY SOUR

Let's forget about sour mix and go back to the basics: A true whiskey sour is not only the template for endless variations, it's a proper classic in its own right. Fresh lemon is essential, and an egg white gently integrates the flavors and contributes a silky texture.

2 oz/60 mL bourbon
1 oz/30 mL lemon juice
¾ oz/20 mL simple syrup
1 fresh egg white

Combine all the ingredients in a cocktail shaker without ice. Shake vigorously for a "dry shake," then add ice and shake again for a "wet shake." Strain into a rocks glass with fresh ice. Garnish with a brandied cherry.

WHISKEY SOUR (NO EGG WHITE)

Even if the thought of raw egg white makes you shudder, I'd encourage you to try a properly made egg white drink at least once; it's all about the texture, with no "eggy" flavor in the least. But if the notion leaves you squeamish, the whiskey sour is still plenty delicious without it.

2 oz/60 mL bourbon
1 oz/30 mL lemon juice
¾ oz/20 mL simple syrup

Combine all the ingredients in a cocktail shaker with ice. Shake until well chilled and strain into a rocks glass with fresh ice. Garnish with a lemon wheel and a brandied cherry.

NEW YORK SOUR

This classic sour variation floats red wine atop the finished drink for a striking two-toned cocktail. A medium-bodied, somewhat fruity red like a Merlot or Malbec will do well here, though traditionally this cocktail used port— if you happen to have ruby port around, have at it!

2 oz/60 mL bourbon
1 oz/30 mL lemon juice
¾ oz/20 mL simple syrup
1 fresh egg white
½ oz/15 mL fruity red wine
   (Merlot or Malbec recommended)

Combine all the ingredients except wine in a cocktail shaker without ice. Shake vigorously for a "dry shake," then add ice and shake again for a "wet shake." Strain into a rocks glass with fresh ice. Carefully float wine over the top.

WHISK(E)Y

To spell with an E, or not an E? In both Europe and North America, we can't seem to agree. In Scotland, Canada, and Japan, it's *whisky*; in Ireland and America, *whiskey*.

HISSY FIT

Josh Ropson, The Vanderbilt

As summer-friendly and drinkable as a bourbon cocktail can get, this drink takes on fruity and floral notes from cassis and St-Germain, while lemon keeps it refreshing rather than overly sweet. A perfect warm-weather party drink.

1½ oz/45 mL Old Grand-Dad bourbon
½ oz/15 mL lemon juice
½ oz/15 mL St-Germain
½ oz/15 mL crème de cassis

Combine all the ingredients in a cocktail shaker with ice. Shake until well chilled and strain into a rocks glass with fresh ice.

Triple Crown, Ba'sik

TWO BITS

David Moo, Quarter Bar

The cool-weather signature cocktail at Quarter Bar, the Two Bits is essentially an Old Fashioned made distinctive through Luxardo amaretto, a sophisticated almond-flavored liqueur that may be far better than amaretto versions you've tried before.

1 oz/30 mL Maker's Mark
1 oz/30 mL Wild Turkey 101 bourbon
¼ oz/10 mL Luxardo amaretto
2 dashes Peychaud's bitters
1 dash Angostura bitters

Combine all the ingredients in a mixing glass with ice. Stir until well chilled and strain into a rocks glass with fresh ice. Garnish with a flamed orange twist (see p. 29).

TRIPLE CROWN

Jay Zimmerman, Ba'sik

A true whiskey sour—spirit, lemon, sugar— has infinite variations; this version plays up the citrus with orangey Montenegro and grapefruit liqueur.

1 oz/30 mL bourbon
¾ oz/20 mL pamplemousse
¾ oz/20 mL lemon juice
¾ oz/20 mL Montenegro amaro

Combine all the ingredients in a cocktail shaker with ice. Shake until well chilled and strain into a coupe. Garnish with a lemon twist.

KINGS COUNTY DISTILLERY

Moonshine—unaged white whiskey—had a true moment in the cocktail world a few years back: partly because of its scrappy, hipster-DIY image; partly because, since it's unaged, upstart distilleries could get it onto the shelves quickly. But Colin Spoelman came by his interest in moonshine from a much more personal direction. "I'm from Kentucky—I grew up in the Appalachian, moonshine part of the state," he says. "I'd go home and get moonshine from bootleggers, which still exist in dry counties in the South. People back in New York were more curious about it than I anticipated. And through their fascination, I grew reinterested in the culture that I came from."

" I'm from Kentucky—I grew up in the Appalachian, moonshine part of the state. "
—Colin Spoelman, Kings County Distillery

In true bootleg fashion, Spoelman started distilling moonshine in his apartment—a slightly obsessive hobby, he called it—before securing a distillery license and opening a true distillery in 2010, before craft distilling had really taken off in the city.

Always intending to produce an aged whiskey as well, Kings County Distillery first entered the market with a white whiskey, while putting more away in barrels. "We wanted to be known as a whiskey distillery, and we wanted to stake out that territory. But I also wanted to argue that age wasn't the only factor of what makes a whiskey good," he says. "It has this outsized importance in the dialogue around whiskey. But other variables—ingredients, fermentation, distillation—matter just as much."

In their case, New York State organic corn serves as the base—"it wasn't ideological, it just happened to make the best whiskey"—as well as malted barley, which Spoelman imports. They distill in a Scottish pot still, which he prefers to a column still for the flexibility and character it allows. "It gives the distiller more latitude in terms of the flavor he's after. With a column still, you can calibrate and spit out the same spirit every time. That's useful if you want the same spirit again and again, but we like to give ourselves more freedom." In addition to the moonshine, Kings County now sells a two-year bourbon, along with an unusual "chocolate whiskey," moonshine infused with cacao bean husks; a four-year bourbon will follow.

KINGS COUNTY DISTILLERY
moonshine
corn whiskey 200ml
40% alcohol by volume

The distillery is housed in the Brooklyn Navy Yards, which the Navy itself left in 1996, leaving the space to become a manufacturing center. "It's an industrial campus, and we're really in a community of people who are producing—whether whiskey, Sweet 'n' Low, movies, or anything else." Craft distilling might sound more hipster Brooklyn than "old New York" Brooklyn. But curiously, their corner of the borough has a distinct moonshine history.

"There were Brooklyn moonshine wars in the late 1860s," he says. "There were raids on illegal Irish whiskey distillers in Dumbo; a revenue officer was shot and killed close to our building. Al Capone was born right across the street from us, and grew up on these mean streets. So somehow, there's a continuity of moonshine history."

Try Kings County's bourbon and moonshine in the following three cocktails.

MARK'S JOHN COLLINS

1½ oz/45 mL Kings County Distillery bourbon
½ oz/15 mL lemon juice
¼ oz/10 mL simple syrup
2 oz/60 mL club soda

Combine all the ingredients in a Collins glass with ice and stir. Top with club soda and garnish with a lemon peel.

THE CHOXIE

1½ oz/45 mL Kings County Distillery moonshine
½ oz/15 mL lemon juice
½ oz/15 mL simple syrup
2 to 3 small cubes of cucumber
Dill

Muddle the cucumber and dill in a cocktail shaker. Add the moonshine, lemon, simple syrup, and ice. Shake until well chilled and double-strain into a rocks glass with fresh ice. Garnish with another sprig of dill.

BOURBON BLUEBERRY CRUMBLE

2 oz/60 mL Kings County Distillery bourbon
½ oz/15 mL blueberry simple syrup
(recipe p. 274)
¼ oz/10 mL Luxardo maraschino liqueur
½ orange slice
10 blueberries

Combine all the ingredients in a cocktail shaker with ice. Shake until well chilled and double-strain into a rocks glass with fresh ice. Garnish with more blueberries.

HAYMAKER'S PUNCH

Del Pedro, Tooker Alley

"This drink is based on something called switchel, also known as 'Haymaker's Punch.' Supposedly it came up from the islands during the colonial American period, and was given to farmhands as a refreshing drink in the fields, particularly in New England," says Del Pedro. "I came across that and said, wow, that's the basis for an amazing sour cocktail."

1¼ oz/40 mL Maker's Mark 46 bourbon
½ oz/15 mL Old Grand-Dad 114 bourbon
¾ oz/20 mL Aperol
¾ oz/20 mL lemon juice
¼ oz/10 mL simple syrup
¼ oz/10 mL cane syrup
  (2:1 raw turbinado sugar to water)
¼ oz/10 mL apple cider vinegar
1 oz/30 mL ginger beer

Combine all the ingredients in a cocktail shaker with ice. Shake until well chilled and strain into a double old fashioned glass with four ice cubes. Garnish with a lemon wedge and candied ginger.

AUTUMN EQUINOX

The Richardson

Any drink becomes immediately autumnal with the addition of allspice dram, an intensely flavored allspice liqueur; bittersweet Braulio amaro backs it up.

2 oz/60 mL Wild Turkey 101 bourbon
¾ oz/20 mL Braulio amaro
¼ oz/10 mL allspice dram

Combine all the ingredients in a mixing glass with ice. Stir until well chilled and strain into a double rocks glass with fresh ice. Garnish with an orange twist.

AMERICAN ROYAL ZEPHYR

Damon Boelte, Grand Army

Damon Boelte's elegant bourbon-Champagne creation riffs off a Seelbach, with Angostura, Peychaud's, and orange bitters playing in the background.

1 oz/30 mL bonded bourbon
1 oz/30 mL Lillet rosé
2 dashes Angostura bitters
2 dashes orange bitters
2 dashes Peychaud's bitters
Champagne

Combine all the ingredients except the Champagne in a mixing glass with ice. Stir until well chilled and strain into a coupe. Top with Champagne and garnish with a cherry.

SMASH OF THE TITANS

Travis St. Germain, Clover Club

Citrus lends itself well to bourbon, as in this vibrant winter sour with a bright burst of kumquat.

2 oz/60 mL Four Roses Yellow Label bourbon
¾ oz/20 mL simple syrup
¼ oz/10 mL lemon juice
4 kumquats
1 sprig of oregano

In the bottom of a cocktail shaker, muddle the kumquats and simple syrup. Add the oregano, bourbon, and lemon juice. Shake until well chilled and pour, ice and all, into a rocks glass. Garnish with two oregano sprigs, one on each side of the glass.

American Royal Zephyr, Grand Army

CLOVER CLUB

In the New York cocktail world, few names command as much respect as Julie Reiner—who has always had a knack for being ahead of the curve. When she moved to New York in 1997, her ingredient-driven, culinary approach to cocktails was highly unusual, in an era of vodka bottle service and Rose's Lime. "At the time, you couldn't get fresh juices to save your life." She quickly caught the attention of the media, and of bar-world legend Dale DeGroff, who led her to realize other bartenders shared her dedication to sophisticated cocktails. When she opened Manhattan's Flatiron Lounge in 2003, "a bar focused solely on high-quality cocktails," there were few others like it. Her next project with mixologist Audrey Saunders, Pegu Club, was a similar hit.

So when Reiner moved to Brooklyn soon after, she immediately saw the need for a craft cocktail bar. Smith Street, the main drag of neighborhood Carroll Gardens, was slowly turning into a restaurant row; but in terms of bars, "There was a hole in what was happening out here." Her aim was a civilized cocktail bar, comfortable and classy. "As opposed to Flatiron, where if people weren't squished up to each other, practically spilling their Beijing Peach cocktails, they weren't happy." Brooklyn was better suited to a different sort of establishment—as was Reiner herself. ("I think you can tell by the bars that I was a little older when I opened Clover," she laughs.)

From the aesthetic to the menu, Reiner was after a pre-Prohibition vibe—"That is, when the cocktail was booming," she says. "There's so much romance around Prohibition, but people were drinking garbage because they couldn't get good booze!" The stately, imposing bar itself was first built in 1897, for a community hall in the coal mining town of Sugar Notch, PA, and it anchors Clover Club's aesthetic: ornate, sophisticated, historically minded.

In keeping with the theme, Reiner's menu serves as something of an encyclopedia of families of mixed drinks. "When we first opened in 2008, customers probably knew what a julep was—but not a smash or a rickey." So the menu is broken out into categories. "We try to give people a little education but still make it fun."

Today, Clover Club's fans hail from all over the city, and thanks to its widespread acclaim, it has no shortage of national and even international visitors. But, according to Reiner, every successful bar is, in essence, a neighborhood bar. "You have to adapt to the neighborhood you're in, and what people want. If you don't do that, you'll fail."

COCKTAIL RECIPES

Clover Club (p. 41)
Gin Blossom (p. 39)
Prospect Park Sour (p. 105)
Smash of the Titans (p. 98)

" When we first opened in 2008, customers probably knew what a julep was—but not a smash or a rickey ... We try to give people a little education but still make it fun. "

—Julie Reiner, Clover Club

ᵒⁿAGING

We all know that an 18-year Scotch will be pricier than a 12-year bottle of the same make. Between evaporation, the risk of leakage, and required storage space, aging whiskey for additional years comes at a considerable cost. But is older whiskey necessarily better?

Let's look at what happens when a spirit ages. Once it's put into a barrel and allowed to rest, the liquid begins to react with the wood, an interplay that contributes all the oaky, vanilla, and caramel flavors we love in brown spirits. But not all spirits age at the same rate. The warmer the temperature, the faster those characteristics emerge. So in the chill, northern climes of Scotland, whisky can age for 12, 15, 18 years; in warmer Kentucky, a 10-year bourbon is on the older end, and 15-year, ancient. Tequila aged in Mexico, quicker still.

So a 12-year bourbon isn't really comparable to a 12-year Scotch. But within a given spirit, is older necessarily better? Not always. To some extent, it's a matter of preference. But some spirits, after years and years in the cask, can grow to taste so much like, well, barrel, that the nuance of the original spirit is lost. The job of a cellarmaster, or a master distiller, is to know exactly when to pull it.

DRINKING AT THE GYM
Ian Hardie, Huckleberry Bar

Bell pepper in a cocktail? Vegetables have indeed found their way into the craft cocktail world: The pepper contributes a distinctive, juicy acidity.

2 oz/60 mL Medley Bros. bourbon
½ oz/15 mL bell pepper syrup (recipe p. 276)
½ oz/15 mL honey syrup
 (2 parts water : 1 part honey)
¾ oz/20 mL lemon juice
1 dash Peychaud's bitters
1 dash Tapatio hot sauce

Combine all the ingredients in a cocktail shaker with ice. Shake until well chilled and double-strain into a rocks glass with one large ice cube. Garnish with an orange twist.

TALENT SCOUT
Brian Smith, Colonie

"A beautiful homage to the Old Fashioned flavor profile," Brian Smith calls this cocktail, which tweaks the bourbon-bitters-citrus formula by using a dry orange liqueur.

2 oz/60 mL Buffalo Trace bourbon
½ oz/15 mL Pierre Ferrand dry Curaçao
2 dashes Angostura bitters
2 dashes orange bitters

Combine all the ingredients in a mixing glass with ice. Stir until well chilled and strain into an Old Fashioned glass with ice. Garnish with an orange twist.

RYE

ARBITRARY NATURE OF TIME

Maks Pazuniak, Jupiter Disco

The spice of rye, bitterness of Campari, balanced sweetness of cherry Heering, and chocolate and spice of mole bitters weave together beautifully in this stirred drink.

1¼ oz/40 mL Wild Turkey 101 rye
1 oz/30 mL Campari
¾ oz/20 mL Heering cherry liqueur
27 drops mole bitters (yes, 27)
1 dash Regan's orange bitters

Combine all the ingredients in a mixing glass with ice. Stir until well chilled and strain into a rocks glass with a big ice cube. Garnish with an orange twist.

PROSPECT PARK SOUR

Brian Farran, Clover Club

A classic sour given a little more body with maple syrup and elusive minty-piney notes from Luxardo's Amaro Abano.

2 oz/60 mL Rittenhouse rye
½ oz/15 mL lemon juice
½ oz/15 mL orange juice
¼ oz/10 mL maple syrup
¼ oz/10 mL Luxardo Amaro Abano

Combine all the ingredients in a cocktail shaker with ice. Shake until well chilled and strain into a sour glass. Garnish with a orange twist.

NEW CEREMONY

Tonia Guffey, Dram

Guffey describes this as a "summer Old Fashioned," with grapefruit liqueur, the wine-based aperitif Byrrh, and a big grapefruit twist on top "which dries the whole thing out."

1 oz/30 mL Rittenhouse rye
½ oz/15 mL Combier pamplemousse rose
½ oz/15 mL Byrrh
½ oz/15 mL Dolin dry vermouth
¼ oz/10 mL Aperol
3 dashes orange bitters

Combine all the ingredients in a mixing glass with ice. Stir until well chilled and strain into a double old fashioned glass with one large ice cube. Garnish with a grapefruit twist.

New Ceremony, Dram

5 TAKES ON THE.... MANHATTAN

"I get really excited about Manhattans," says David Moo of Quarter Bar. "I love that drink. I love making them. I love drinking them. A mediocre Manhattan is like pizza; even if it's only okay, it's still pretty good."

Along with the similarly composed Martini (both follow the template of spirit + vermouth), it's one of the foundational cocktails in the canon. And, to this day, it's a way to gauge a bartender's abilities. "How a bar handles a Manhattan really tells you

something about that bar," says Moo—about technique, professionalism, attention to detail. With only two essential ingredients, details matter. "When I teach our bartenders how to make Manhattans, it imparts a whole set of principles."

DAVID MOO, QUARTER BAR

"For our Manhattan, we add a couple little moves. We put bitters in the empty glass, then express orange and lemon peels. We use those peels to spread the bitters around the inside of the cocktail glass before pouring the drink in, which suffuses the whole cocktail with an extra subtle note of citrus oil and bitters."

2½ oz/75 mL Old Overholt rye
½ oz/15 mL Martini & Rossi sweet vermouth
½ oz/15 mL Carpano Antica Formula sweet vermouth
3 dashes Angostura bitters
1 orange peel
1 lemon peel

To a chilled coupe, add a dash of Angostura bitters. Twist one orange peel and one lemon peel into the glass. Rub the peels around the glass in the citrus oils and bitters, to spread over the inside of the glass, then discard peels. Combine all other ingredients in a mixing glass with ice. Stir until well chilled. Strain cocktail into the prepared glass. Garnish with a brandied cherry.

ALLEN KATZ, NY DISTILLING CO.

"I use two different vermouths for a Manhattan; Carpano is round and rich, whereas Punt e Mes contributes earthiness and spice."

2 oz/60 mL Ragtime rye
½ oz/15 mL Carpano Antica Formula sweet vermouth
½ oz/15 mL Punt e Mes vermouth
1 dash Angostura bitters

Combine all the ingredients in a mixing glass with ice. Stir until well chilled and strain into a chilled coupe. Garnish with a brandied cherry.

RAISIN THE BAR
DARREN GRENIA,
YOURS SINCERELY

This raisin-infused Manhattan recipe was developed for the bar Yours Sincerely, where Grenia puts the drink on tap. Here's a scaled-down variation to make at home.

2 oz/60 mL Raisin Rye
(recipe p. 267)
¼ oz/10 mL Dolin dry vermouth
¼ oz/10 mL Cocchi Torino
sweet vermouth
1 dash Angostura bitters

Combine all ingredients in a mixing glass with ice. Stir until well chilled and strain into a coupe. Garnish with a rye-infused raisin.

MANHATTANITE
DEL PEDRO,
TOOKER ALLEY

Vermouth swaps out for similarly sweet, wine-based aperitif Dubonnet Rouge, and tweaks the formula with a sparing measure of orange liqueur.

2 oz/60 mL Rittenhouse rye
1 oz/30 mL Dubonnet Rouge
1 tsp Cointreau
2 dashes of orange bitters

Combine all the ingredients in a mixing glass with cracked ice cubes. Stir until well chilled and strain into a Nick and Nora glass. Garnish with a flamed orange peel (see p. 29).

SOUTH OF MANHATTAN
DAVID SHERIDAN,
WHEATED

From Ditmas Park pizzeria and cocktail bar Wheated, here bourbon pairs with Cardamaro, which, like sweet vermouth, is rich and wine-based (but unlike vermouth, qualifies as an amaro).

2 oz/60 mL bourbon
1 oz/30 mL Cardamaro amaro
6 drops of Hamilton 7 Year
Old St. Lucia Pot Still rum or
another aged rum

Combine all the ingredients in a mixing glass with ice. Stir until well chilled and strain into a coupe. Garnish with a cherry.

MAURICE
ST. JOHN FRIZELL,
FORT DEFIANCE

St. John Frizell's Maurice may be in the rye-vermouth-bitter camp, but in this case, the role of "bitter" is assumed by the powerful gentian liqueur Amère Sauvage, and gently lightened by the aperitif Cocchi Americano.

1½ oz/45 mL Rittenhouse rye
¾ oz/20 mL Cocchi Americano
½ oz/15 mL Carpano Antica
Formula sweet vermouth
¼ oz/10 mL Bittermens
Amère Sauvage

Combine all the ingredients in a mixing glass with ice. Stir until well chilled and strain into a coupe. Garnish with a lemon twist.

BROOKLYN

How could a book about Brooklyn cocktails leave out the Brooklyn itself? A descendant of the Manhattan, its whiskey and vermouth—though dry vermouth, rather than sweet—are supported by maraschino liqueur and, traditionally, Amer Picon. Given that that liqueur is exceedingly difficult to track down in the States, try substituting Averna plus extra orange bitters to replicate Amer Picon's bitter-orangey character.

2 oz/60 mL rye
1 oz/30 mL dry vermouth
¼ oz/10 mL Luxardo maraschino
¼ oz/10 mL Averna
4 dashes orange bitters

Combine all the ingredients in a mixing glass with ice. Stir until well chilled and strain into a rocks glass with ice. Garnish with a lemon twist.

NEW RIDER

Christa Manalo, Rucola

Rye shines in stirred, boozy drinks, but can pick up lighter flavors as well, as in this sour with ginger and the excellent cherry liqueur Luxardo maraschino.

1 oz/30 mL rye
1 oz/30 mL lemon juice
½ oz/15 mL Luxardo maraschino
½ oz/15 mL ginger syrup (recipe p. 273)
3 dashes Angostura bitters

Combine all the ingredients in a cocktail shaker with ice. Shake until well chilled and strain into a coupe. Garnish with a sage leaf.

À LA LOUISIANE

Maison Premiere

A classic derived from the Manhattan, with complex earthy-herbal bitter notes thanks to Benedictine, absinthe, and anise-heavy Peychaud's bitters.

1¾ oz/50 mL Rittenhouse rye
¾ oz/20 mL Carpano Antica Formula sweet vermouth
½ oz/15 mL Benedictine
4 dashes absinthe
4 dashes Peychaud's bitters

Combine all the ingredients in a mixing glass with ice. Stir until well chilled and strain into a coupe. Garnish with a skewered cherry.

RATTLESNAKE

An aptly named cocktail, with a surprise bite from absinthe. Some versions add a few drops of absinthe to the cocktail, but an absinthe rinse works equally well.

2 oz/60 mL rye
¾ oz/20 mL lemon juice
½ oz/15 mL simple syrup
1 egg white
Absinthe

Rinse a coupe glass with absinthe by pouring a very small amount into the bottom of the glass, swirling around to coat, then discarding. Combine all the other ingredients in a cocktail shaker without ice. Shake vigorously for a "dry shake," then add ice and shake again. Strain into the prepared coupe.

THE TRUCE

Torrey Bell-Edwards, Willow

"What started as a maple-chartreuse Sazerac evolved into an Old Pal–esque drink that, despite its seriously boozy components, remains very quaffable," says Bell-Edwards.

2 oz/60 mL High West Double rye
¼ oz/10 mL green Chartreuse
¼ oz/10 mL maple syrup
¼ oz/10 mL dry vermouth

Combine all the ingredients in a mixing glass and stir until well chilled. Strain into a rocks glass with one large ice cube, and garnish with a twist of lemon on the cube.

THE PHENOMENON of the PICKLEBACK

A shot of whiskey, and a shot of ... pickle juice? Whether that sounds appealing or revolting is a matter of taste, but there's no denying that the "pickleback"—as this unlikely duo is called—has found a real following in Brooklyn. It first came to be at the Bushwick Country Club (p. 119; not, in fact, a country club) in 2006. McClure's Pickles, now a national brand, had just gotten its start two doors down on their Williamsburg street, and was storing pickles in BCC's basement. "One day our bartender Reggie was sitting on the bar, totally hung over, snacking on pickles from downstairs," BCC owner John Roberts said, "and a girl came in and asked if she could drink some of the pickle brine. He said fine, "but only if you do a shot of Old Crow with me first." Bourbon first, a pickle brine chaser—and thus the pickleback was born. The next day, "There was a gaggle of regulars at the end of the bar who had had quite a few; I thought they were crazy, but then I tasted it. Wow, do those go down easy."

Friends at other New York bars picked up the pickleback, which spread throughout the city, and then worldwide. "It's in Tokyo, it's in Paris. One of our old employees was backpacking through Central America, and in a middle-of-nowhere bar that was actually a treehouse, she saw a sign: *Try the pickleback.*"

Improbable though it might sound, there's an underlying logic to the pickleback. A Bloody Mary, after all, is an essentially savory drink; a dirty martini stirs olive brine right in there with the vodka. So savory flavors and booze are nothing new. Acidity is a key element in cocktails, and nothing matches the vinegar hit of pickle brine for acidity. And the no-nonsense pickleback, in a sense, is the antithesis of overly ornate cocktails—what's more proudly lowbrow than pickles and cheap whiskey?

THE ORIGINAL PICKLEBACK

Shot of Old Crow bourbon
Shot of McClure's Spicy Pickle brine

Shoot the bourbon and chase it with the pickle brine. Repeat at your own risk.

John Roberts, Bushwick Country Club

CAULFIELD'S DREAM
The Narrows

From the Bushwick bar's opening menu, this sour uses rich, brown demerara sugar syrup as its sweetener, paired with mint and lemon, two of whiskey's best friends.

1½ oz/45 mL Old Overholt rye
¾ oz/20 mL lemon juice
¾ oz/20 mL demerara syrup (1:1)
1 dash Angostura bitters
4 to 5 mint leaves
Cava

Combine all the ingredients except the cava in a cocktail shaker with ice. Shake until well chilled and double-strain into a coupe. Top with a splash of cava.

Jacques and Doris, Fort Defiance

SCOTCH

CAVE CREEK
Nate Dumas, The Shanty

Some cocktails don't use Scotch as a base in itself, but part of a split base with less smoky, aggressive whiskeys.

1¼ oz/40 mL Mister Katz's Rock and Rye
1 oz/30 mL Pig's Nose Scotch whisky
¾ oz/20 mL lemon juice
½ oz/15 mL grenadine (recipe p. 19)
¼ oz/10 mL Campari
Club soda

Combine all the ingredients except club soda in a cocktail shaker with ice. Shake until well chilled and strain into a Collins glass filled with fresh ice. Top with chilled club soda and garnish with a lemon twist. Serve with a straw.

JACQUES AND DORIS
Tyler Caffall, Fort Defiance

Riffing on a Sazerac, Tyler Caffall rinses a cocktail glass with herbaceous liqueur Suze (rather than absinthe), the vessel for a stirred drink with powerful Islay whisky Laphroaig backed up by blended Scotch and stirred with ample Peychaud's bitters.

1¼ oz/40 mL Bank Note Scotch whisky
(or other blended Scotch)
¾ oz/20 mL Laphroaig Scotch whisky
⅜ oz/12 mL Sirop J.M
4 dashes Peychaud's bitters
1 dash lavender bitters
Suze

Rinse or mist a small, chilled rocks glass with Suze. Combine all the other ingredients in a mixing glass and stir until well chilled. Strain into the prepared glass without ice. Twist a grapefruit peel over the top, then discard.

ON COCKTAIL NAMES

M ost chefs don't name the dishes on their menu. (An heirloom tomato salad is generally called, well, an heirloom tomato salad.) But naming cocktails is part of a bartender's gig, just as musicians have to name their songs. There are punny names and literal ones, historically-minded cocktail names and repurposed album titles—and some that are just off the wall.

Extra Fancy is king of the punny cocktail names—but not only for the bartenders' own amusement. "The name is the hook," says general manager Meaghan Montagano. "When you read through a cocktail menu, it catches your eye; it leads you to think, *What is that?* If it's funny or quirky or memorable, it just draws you in."

For co-owner Rob Krueger, names have the opportunity to reflect the bar's own culture and personality. "A lot of times, names just come from something that's said, and you need to grab it in the moment," he says.

"Keeping your mind open and generating ideas is part of the process," says Krueger. "We have fun here, and if the drink is fun, everyone's pitching in ideas and eventually something sticks."

SAZERAC
St. John Frizell, Fort Defiance

"I love a Sazerac. It's a charming drink; it's probably my favorite drink to make," says St. John Frizell of the enduring classic. "It's such a weird presentation"—served in a rocks glass, sans ice—"It almost should be served up but it's not, and there's no reason why. Tradition, I guess."

2 oz/60 mL Old Overholt rye
¼ oz/10 mL simple syrup
2 dashes Peychaud's bitters
1 dash Angostura bitters
Pernod Absinthe

Rinse or mist a small, chilled rocks glass with absinthe. Combine all the other ingredients in a mixing glass and stir until well chilled. Strain into the prepared glass without ice. Twist a lemon peel over the top, then discard.

FAITH AND FORTITUDE
Ian Hardie, Huckleberry Bar

How does a brawny, smoky Scotch like Ardbeg translate to a lively shaken drink? With the addition of lemon, cucumber, and velvet falernum—a spiced lime-almond-ginger-clove syrup commonly used in tiki drinks.

1 oz/30 mL Ardbeg Scotch whisky
1 oz/30 mL velvet falernum
½ oz/15 mL lemon juice
¼ oz/10 mL cucumber syrup (recipe p. 276)
3 dashes Angostura bitters

Combine all the ingredients in a cocktail shaker with ice. Shake until well chilled and double-strain into a rocks glass with one large ice cube. Garnish with a lemon twist.

THE SHANTY

What better way to showcase the spirits of a Brooklyn distillery, than to build a cocktail bar right inside. "The Shanty was always part of the fantasy," says Allen Katz, of New York Distilling Co. (page X), "as long as we could find a space to accommodate it." After more than 40 site visits, he and his partners discovered a suitable building—spacious enough to house a distillery and a bar, on the outskirts of burgeoning Williamsburg.

With a relaxed, industrial feel, The Shanty is an attractive bar in its own right, but one look through the glass wall that separates it from the [production area], and guests are face-to-face with the barrels and stills that produce every drop of New York Distilling's gins and ryes. "We want guests to come in, relax, have a good time—and if you're interested in our spirits we'll tell you everything about them."

Nate Dumas works their spirits into many clever cocktails, including the pleasantly bitter Sauvetage (p. X), the 700 Songs Gimlet (p. X), and some that take the unusual step of combining whiskey and gin, such as the Double Standard Sour (p. x).

Of course many cocktails feature the house whiskeys and gins, but the intention was never to exclude other brands. "You don't walk in here and feel beaten over the head, Please drink our spirits!," says Katz. With over 200 bottles behind the bar, New York Distilling's products are featured, but hardly dominate. "If you want a tequila drink, or a rum drink, it's our great pleasure."

COCKTAIL RECIPES

Cave Creek (p. 110)
Big Iron (p. 123)
Sauvetage (p. 43)
Cannibal Corpse Reviver #2 (p. 43)
700 Songs Gimlet (p. 52)

" We want guests to come in, relax, have a good time— and if you're interested in our spirits we'll tell you everything about them. "

—Nate Dumas, The Shanty

“ You don't walk in here and feel beaten over the head, 'Please drink our spirits!' If you want a tequila drink, or a rum drink, it's our great pleasure. ”

—*Allen Katz, The Shanty*

TAKES ON THE JULEP

The julep is one of the earliest American classics on record, dating back to the 18th century. These days, bourbon is the julep standard, but brandy and rum juleps were popular throughout the pre-Prohibition era.

CLASSIC MINT JULEP

Key for a classic mint julep: Don't muddle the mint into a pulp, the way you'd smash up ginger or apple, say. Just gently press it—a massage, not a pounding—to release its flavor.

2 oz/60 mL bourbon
8 to 10 mint leaves
½ oz/15 mL simple syrup

In a julep cup or rocks glass, *gently* press the mint and ¼ oz/10 mL of the simple syrup with a muddler. Add the remaining ¼ oz/10 mL of simple syrup and the bourbon. Fill the cup with crushed ice. Garnish with a mint bouquet and a short straw.

MENTA MAKE A JULEP

ALLISON KAVE, BUTTER & SCOTCH

This julep forgoes mint in its base for the powerful amaro Branca Menta, perhaps mint-ier than mint itself.

2 oz/60 mL Old Overholt rye
½ oz/15 mL molasses simple syrup (recipe p. 272)
¼ oz/10 mL Branca Menta

Combine the rye and molasses syrup in a rocks glass or julep tin. Fill the cup with crushed ice, then drizzle with the Branca Menta. Garnish with a mint sprig and a stirrer.

SMOKE & MIRROR

ARNAUD DISSAIS, LOOSIE ROUGE

Delicate, herbaceous shiso leaves take the place of mint in this bourbon julep, with a spritz of ultrasmoky Laphroaig single-malt Scotch for a surprising additional element.

2 oz/60 mL Bulleit bourbon
½ oz/15 mL lemon juice
½ oz/15 mL honey syrup (2 honey : 1 water)
Laphroaig Scotch
4 shiso leaves

In the bottom of a julep tin, gently muddle the shiso leaves. Add the bourbon, lemon juice, honey syrup, and three sprays of Laphroaig (or a few drops, if a mister is not available). Fill the tin with crushed ice and garnish with another shiso leaf.

BARBER OF SEVILLE

WILL ELLIOTT, MAISON PREMIERE

"People see this on the menu and think it'll be a rye drink, but it's really a sherry drink," says Will Elliott. The bulk of this refreshing low-proof julep is light, aromatic Manzanilla sherry and wine-based aperitif Cappelletti. (The elaborate garnish is more than a little involved, but creates a clever "sandy beach" effect atop the crushed ice.)

1 oz/30 mL Hidalgo Manzanilla sherry
¾ oz/20 mL Cappelletti
½ oz/15 mL Old Overholt rye
½ oz/15 mL lemon
¼ oz/10 mL orgeat
¼ tsp orange flower water
3 dashes orange bitters

Combine all the ingredients in a julep tin. Fill the tin with crushed ice. Insert two short straws or sip sticks. Maison Premiere garnishes with a parasol, very long, thin strings of orange peel, and shaved Marcona almonds.

Barber of Seville, Maison Premiere

IRISH WHISKEY

INFERNAL AFFAIRS

Jeremy Oertel, Donna

Peated whiskeys generally hail from Scotland, but Connemara produces a unique peated Irish whiskey in the style of a single malt. It's paired with much mellower Irish Tullamore Dew for a fascinating sour that brings in flavors of apple and ginger.

1½ oz/45 mL Tullamore D.E.W. Irish whiskey
½ oz/15 mL Connemara Peated Irish whiskey
1 oz/30 mL Fuji apple juice
¾ oz/20 mL lemon juice
½ oz/15 mL ginger syrup (recipe p. 273)
1 dash Jerry Thomas' Own Decanter bitters

Combine all the ingredients in a cocktail shaker with ice. Shake until well chilled and strain into a coupe.

MCGEE'S NUT WARMER

Grand Ferry Tavern

Smooth, sophisticated Redbreast is an ideal backdrop for Nocino, a distinctive green walnut liqueur.

1 oz/30 mL Redbreast 12 Year Old whiskey
1 oz/30 mL Dolin sweet vermouth
1 oz/30 mL Nocino walnut liqueur

Combine all the ingredients in a mixing glass with ice. Stir until well chilled and strain into a chilled coupe.

BUSHWICK COUNTRY CLUB

To understand Bushwick Country Club, or BCC, first know this: The name is *strictly* tongue-in-cheek. "It is funny when people call, thinking that we're an actual country club," says owner John Roberts. The laid-back bar does have "membership cards," thanks to "a joke that got out of hand," according to Roberts. (One BCC card-carrying member once talked himself into a Houston country club—claiming that his club had reciprocity.)

Nor is the bar itself in Bushwick—rather, it's in neighboring Williamsburg. But thanks to a zoning quirk, the backyard and its miniature golf course is, in fact, zoned as Bushwick.

Yes, miniature golf. "From the very beginning, mini-golf was always part of the plan," says Roberts, who came up with the idea at a mini-golf course on the Jersey Shore, where he wished there could be a bar every third hole. "Mini-golf and drinking just go together. Like chocolate and peanut butter."

That fun-loving attitude pervades the bar, from the Big Buck Hunter video game machines to the jukebox and pirate flags on the walls. "A regular once said to me, 'I feel like I'm at a house party where someone's parents are out of town,'" says Roberts.

Not a cocktail bar in the least (though several bartenders also work at much higher-end bars, with Bushwick Country Club as a more relaxed night in their schedule), the bar does have several drinks of note. There's a slushy machine, freezing up sweet tea vodka slushies,

and Jim Beam & Coke. ("I had that idea when I was much younger, pouring whiskey into Slurpees from 7-11.") But BCC permanently established its place in drinking history by accidentally inventing the pickleback—a shot of whiskey followed by a shot of pickle brine, which has been a hipster sensation for years.

It's the kind of bar where anything can happen, for better or worse. "There are at least twelve couples who first met here," says Roberts, "and those are just the ones I know of." And he clearly relishes the experience. "My job is to make people walk out happy—and I feel really lucky that I get to do that."

COCKTAIL RECIPES

Pickleback (p. 109)

**❝ My job is to make people walk out happy—
and I feel really lucky that I get to do that. ❞**

—*John Roberts, Bushwick Country Club*

3

TAKES ON THE OLD FASHIONED

What earned the Old Fashioned its title? Once upon a time, the definition of a cocktail was much more specific than in today's anything-goes era. Spirit, sugar, water, bitters. So as cocktails continued to evolve, and some drinkers fondly recalled the drinks of yore, they'd request a cocktail in the "old-fashioned" manner—and the name stuck.

"When you make [people] a clean, proper cocktail, it's received so well."
—Ian Hardie, Huckleberry Bar.

And a true Old Fashioned really is that simple. (Note that you don't see "muddled oranges and cherries" anywhere in that definition.) Spirit: generally bourbon or rye, if not otherwise specified—though just about any spirit, particularly brown spirits, can be Old Fashioned-ified. Sugar, either as a sugar cube or simple syrup. Water, in the form of ice melt as that cocktail gets stirred. And bitters: Angostura is often, but not always, preferred. A twist of citrus as a garnish, or with the peel (not the fruit) gently muddled in the cocktail. And there you have it.

"People can be surprised, if they've had Old Fashioneds that look like a fruit salad in the bottom of the glass. When you make them a clean, proper cocktail, it's received so well," says Ian Hardie of Huckleberry Bar.

KEITH KENJI COCHRAN,
THE NARROWS

"We learned this method from cocktail historian David Wondrich, who's been a friend of our bar for years," says Keith Kenji Cochran.

2 oz/60 mL Rittenhouse rye
1 large demerara sugar cube
2 dashes Angostura bitters
1 thin strip of orange peel

In the bottom of a mixing glass, thoroughly muddle the sugar together with the Angostura bitters. Add the orange peel (*not* the orange fruit), and muddle again to press oils into the sugar mixture. Add the rye and ice to the glass and stir until well chilled. Strain into a rocks glass with fresh ice. Garnish with an orange twist and a dash of orange bitters.

TONIA GUFFEY,
DRAM

"We always use high-proof whiskey; Evan Williams Bottled in Bond if you want bourbon; Rittenhouse if you want rye. (I prefer everything with rye.) It comes out being the perfect balance of sweet and citrus."

2 oz/60 mL Rittenhouse rye
or Evan Williams Bottled
in Bond bourbon
¼ oz/10 mL rich demerara
syrup (2 parts sugar to
1 part water)
2 dashes orange bitters
2 dashes Angostura bitters

Combine all the ingredients in a mixing glass with several cracked ice cubes. Stir until well chilled and strain into a rocks glass with one large ice cube. Garnish with an expressed orange peel and an expressed lemon peel.

BIG IRON
NATE DUMAS,
THE SHANTY

Rock and Rye was a popular spirit in pre-Prohibition days, but languished in obscurity until New York Distilling Co. revived it in 2014. Essentially rye sweetened with rock sugar (plus, in their case, cherry and cinnamon), it's halfway to an Old Fashioned already; just add bitters and ice.

2 oz/60 mL Mister Katz's
Rock and Rye
1 dash Angostura bitters
1 dash orange bitters

Combine all the ingredients in a rocks glass with one large ice cube. Stir until well chilled and serve.

DONNA

RUM AND CACHAÇA

T oo many drinkers hear "rum" and immediately think ". . . and Coke." Or associate it with cloying, syrupy sweetness; or oversugared frozen vacation drinks. Distilled from fermented sugar cane (usually molasses), rum can of course be sweeter than many other liquors. But it's also one of the most adaptable, nuanced, cocktail-friendly spirits out there.

"In some ways, rum is still waiting for its moment," says Matt Belanger of Donna. "But it's versatile, and helps you make great cocktails with a lot of complexity. And it's cost-effective, too; you can get amazing rums really cheap."

A good white rum, not too harsh and not too sweet, is as mixable a spirit as vodka or gin, while a years-old *añejo* can have the barrel-aged character of a whiskey. And made all over the Caribbean, Latin America and beyond, rum is also a spirit with a true sense of place; a Jamaican rum hardly resembles a Nicaraguan rum, which in turn differs from a Cuban.

And at the high end, some aged rums rival fine whiskeys in quality; many bartenders consider them among the best spirits in the world. "Plenty of people who drink Woodford Reserve turn their nose up at a 15-year rum," says Leif Huckman of Donna. Their loss.

DONNA

The southwest fringe of Williamsburg is hardly tropical, but stepping into Donna might have you feel otherwise. "We always wanted this to be an oasis," says owner Leif Huckman, whose mother hails from Honduras; he sought to create a space that spoke to a Latin American breezy, open vibe. The space that houses Donna was previously an antiques store, but according to Huckman, already felt like a bar—"and in fact, it had been a sailors' flophouse in the 1850s," he says. "I totally fell in love with the place and the story behind it."

> **"We take our cocktails very seriously, but since we take it seriously, other people can have fun."** —Leif Huckman, Donna

Huckman and the team he recruited, beverage director Jeremy Oertel and head bartender Matt Belanger, didn't want to imitate the prevailing bar trend circa 2011—the closed-off speakeasy. "At the time, the cocktail bars of the highest caliber had a sort of kitsch factor, dark and masculine-feeling and, at times I thought, overwrought," says Huckman. Donna is open and airy, a white interior with vaulted ceilings and lazy fans—very much the antithesis of such closed-feeling, intimidating bars.

With the menu, too, there's a sense of lightheartedness. "We like to have fun and be a little playful," says Jeremy Oertel. "We're not doing sixty-five drinks like some cocktail bars out there. We want to hit certain notes, and appeal to a wide variety of people, without going crazy." Belanger agrees. "There are some cocktail bars where you look at the listed ingredients and think, *What does this actually taste like?*" Their menu breaks down the list by category: some cocktails light-bodied and approachable; others, full-bodied and complex. "We actually want people to end up with a drink they want."

Rum is a mainstay of the cocktail menu; "It fit the vibe of the place," says Oertel, "and the atmosphere of it—that Central American feeling. It's one of my favorite spirits, and one of Matt's." And while Donna is by no means a tiki bar, a number of drinks do have clear tiki influence, again in keeping with the bar's oasislike aesthetic.

Though the cocktails are complex, they're intended to be as approachable as Donna itself. "We take our cocktails very seriously," says Huckman, "but since we take it seriously, other people can have fun." One taste of a Brancolada—slushy, creamy, like the world's best milkshake crossed with a sophisticated modern-day cocktail—explains that philosophy perfectly.

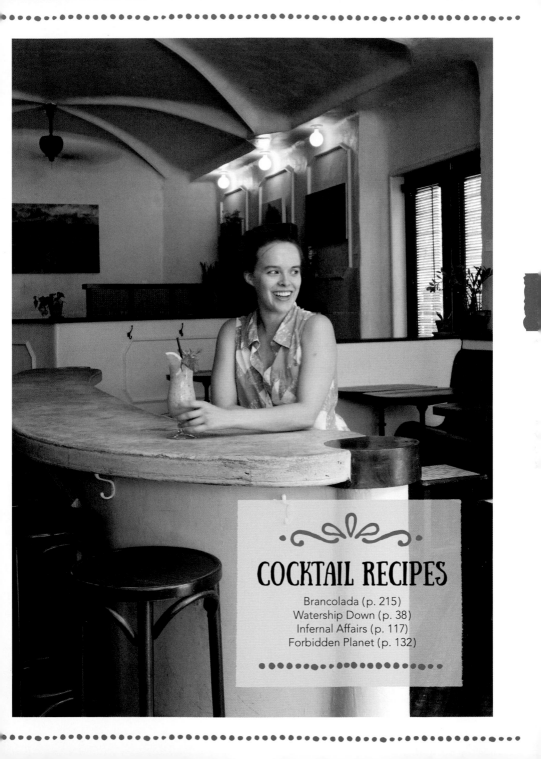

COCKTAIL RECIPES

" [Rum] fit the vibe of the place . . . and the atmosphere of it—that Central American feeling. It's one of my favorite spirits, and one of Matt's. **"** —*Jeremy Oertel, Donna*

WOODY GUTHRIE

Del Pedro, Tooker Alley

Rum pairs perfectly with autumnal flavors—apple, apple cider, ginger, and pear brandy—in this easy-to-guzzle tall drink.

1¾ oz/50 mL El Dorado 12 Year rum
¼ oz/10 mL Clear Creek Pear brandy
¾ oz/20 mL lemon juice
½ oz/15 mL simple syrup
¼ oz/10 mL cane syrup
  (2:1 raw turbinado sugar to water)
1 oz/30 mL fresh apple cider
¾ oz/20 mL ginger beer
¼ Macintosh apple
1 dash Angostura bitters

In the bottom of a cocktail shaker, muddle the apple with the lemon juice and simple syrup. Add ice and all the remaining ingredients except the cider and shake until well chilled. Pour the cider into a highball glass with ice. Strain the cocktail on top. Garnish with an apple slice and candied ginger.

Woody Guthrie, Tooker Alley

THE KICKSTARTER

Blueprint

Gosling's is best known for the Dark and Stormy, but this sweet, full-bodied rum can pair with other ingredients as well; it stands up to espresso in this pick-me-up cocktail from Park Slope bar Blueprint.

2 oz/60 mL Gosling's rum
1 oz/30 mL espresso
½ oz/15 mL turbinado syrup (1:1)
1 dash coffee bitters

Combine all the ingredients in a cocktail shaker with ice. Shake until well chilled and strain into a chilled coupe. Garnish with a twist of lemon.

KING'S TOWN PUNCH

David Moo, Quarter Bar

A sophisticated take on generally fruity "rum punches," this version is built from a base of hibiscus tea, or *agua de jamaica*, a fragrant base for the rum, lime, and bitters.

1 oz/30 mL gold rum
¾ oz/20 mL Gosling's Black Seal rum
¼ oz/10 mL lime juice
1 tsp simple syrup
1 short dash Fee Whiskey
  Barrel-Aged bitters
1 short dash A.B. Smeby
  Hibiscus Rose bitters
Agua de jamaica (recipe p. 283)

In a highball glass with ice, combine all the ingredients except the agua de jamaica and stir well. Add agua de jamaica to fill.

DECODING TIKI

In some ways, tiki drinks seem like the antithesis of modern craft cocktails—at least their first wave. Flamboyant where many classics are austere, often sweet and fruity where many classics are all about the spirits, a product of fairly recent pop culture— there's plenty to regard with suspicion.

But tiki has its own fascinating history in the drinking world, and in the last few years, cocktail enthusiasts have found endless material to mine and refashion. Founding father Ernest Gantt (who later changed his name to Donn Beach) was a world traveler in his youth, who became infatuated with the South Pacific and the Caribbean—two wholly distinct and in many ways, dissimilar regions, to be sure—from their spirits to their fruits to their native artistry. When he opened a bar and restaurant called Don the Beachcomber in 1933, he brought together all these elements, with nautical and tropical decor, "Polynesian" (if largely Cantonese- derived) cuisine, and fruity, potent rum cocktails (sound familiar?). The place became a hit and Donn expanded to new locations, while Victor Bergeron, known as "Trader Vic," opened his own similar chain, beginning in northern California.

Between the two of them, "Don" and "Vic" launched the tiki movement, with endless imitators who picked up on the trend, particularly in the post-WWII era. Tiki drinks were defined by their heavy use of rum, from funky-complex Jamaican rums to overproof 151 to thick, syrupy Blackstrap—perhaps all in the same drink. In the competitive bar landscape, syrups and mixes were jealously guarded proprietary formulas. And as escapism was always part of the tiki ethos—a tropical vacation, without the vacation—tiki was largely about *fun*; garnishes were elaborate and ornate, drinks were ample, the theme was all-in.

Tiki classics named Mai Tais and Zombies, in the ensuing decades, have evolved as sickly sweet, often off-putting drinks. But in recent years, craft bartenders have returned to tiki's roots—whether cocktails that originated with the tiki founding fathers, or the drinking traditions that originally inspired them.

"It's funny because in its way, a tiki bar is a very fake thing, incredibly inauthentic," says Matt Belanger of Donna. "It's a pastiche, a mid-century American way of just misappropriating all this other stuff and not giving a shit about where it actually comes from." To some bartenders, that's part of the fun; to others, it's an interesting perspective through which to view rum drinks: through the source material, as it were. Says Belanger; "We're more interested in where this stuff actually originated."

Today, you'll find tiki bars in a number of major cities. But far more bars, including many in Brooklyn, have simply taken tiki as one aspect of what they do—from a number of loosely tiki-inspired drinks on the menu at Donna, to a monthly drink on the menu at Dram, to the full-fledged weekly tiki cocktail menu every Thursday at Fort Defiance.

SURFLINER
DAMON BOELTE,
GRAND ARMY

A true believer in the elaborate excess of tiki—with some of the best tiki mugs and accessories imaginable—Damon Boelte brings together classic flavors along with smoky, slightly funky Smith & Cross Jamaican rum.

1½ oz/45 mL Smith & Cross rum
½ oz/15 mL blue Curaçao
¾ oz/20 mL pineapple juice
½ oz/15 mL lime juice
½ oz/15 mL toasted orgeat
3 dashes allspice dram
Angostura bitters

Combine the first six ingredients in a cocktail shaker with three ice cubes, and shake back and forth several times. Strain over crushed ice in a wine glass, and top with several dashes of the Angostura bitters. Garnish with a pineapple wedge and a pineapple leaf.

FORBIDDEN PLANET
MATTHEW BELANGER,
DONNA

This cocktail illustrates the bar's tendency to build off—but deviate from—the tiki tradition; frequent tiki players lime, orgeat, falernum, and coconut come together with an original green tea–infused rum.

1¾ oz/50 mL Genmaicha green tea rum (recipe p. 267)
¼ oz/10 mL Wray and Nephew Jamaican rum
1 oz/30 mL lime juice
¾ oz/20 mL orgeat
1 tsp velvet falernum
½ tsp Kalani coconut liqueur
1 dash Angostura bitters

Combine all the ingredients in a cocktail shaker with ice. Shake until well chilled and strain into a coupe. Garnish with a lime wheel.

SERGEANT MAJOR

KATE O'CONNOR
MORRIS, ROSE'S

This tiki-style cocktail counters its tropical sweetness with a modern touch, a float of the powerfully herbal-bitter aperitif Contratto Bitter.

1½ oz/45 mL Diplomático Reserva rum
½ oz/15 mL lime juice
½ oz/15 mL dry Curaçao
¾ oz/20 mL Contratto Bitter
3 1-inch/25-mm pineapple cubes

In the bottom of a cocktail shaker, muddle the pineapple. Add the rum, lime, Curaçao, and ice and shake until well chilled. Strain into a tall glass with crushed ice. Float the Contratto Bitter on top.

NAVY GROG

JOHN BUSH, TALDE

This version of a Don the Beachcomber drink simplifies the original recipe considerably while keeping the basic formula: rum, lime, grapefruit, honey. A lime slice is a necessary garnish; a lime slice with an American flag toothpick stuck into it, even better.

2 oz/60 mL El Dorado Light rum
1 oz/30 mL grapefruit juice
¾ oz/20 mL lime juice
1 oz/30 mL honey syrup (1:1)
½ oz/15 mL Kraken rum

Combine the first four ingredients in a cocktail shaker with ice. Shake until well chilled and strain into a rocks glass with ice. Float the Kraken rum on top. Garnish with a lime slice.

TIKI GLOSSARY

ORGEAT: A nonalcoholic almond syrup scented with orange flower water

VELVET FALERNUM: a Caribbean spiced syrup, either nonalcoholic or low in alcohol, flavored with almond, ginger, clove, and lime

CURAÇAO: a Caribbean orange liqueur

GRENADINE: a reduced pomegranate syrup used in many classics beyond tiki (recipe p. 19)

"DONN'S MIX": a closely guarded secret recipe, essential to many of Don the Beachcomer's drinks—now known to be grapefruit and cinnamon syrup

TOOKER ALLEY

To talk to Del Pedro about his bartending career is to appreciate the last 30-odd years of New York bartending history. A Bermuda native, Pedro came to New York in 1982, and like so many fellow artists and musicians, took up bartending to support a musical career.

He made his way through every kind of establishment, from a dive bar in then-dicey Harlem ("all construction workers and meatpackers and criminals") to sophisticated restaurant bars. He always had an interest in classic, historical cocktails, but saw that as a hobby wholly divorced from his day-to-day bartending. "I felt like I had found this dead art, but none of the other bartenders were that interested." But by 1996, he came to Grange Hall, then one of the few bars with an ambitious cocktail program; "I was with these other weirdos, obsessed with the same stuff I was."

Cocktail culture evolved dramatically over the years, and Pedro's "PhD in mixology," as he puts it, began when his friend Audrey Saunders recruited him to work at Pegu Club, one of the most influential bars of the mid-2000s. It was a steep learning curve, to say the least. "I was kind of pissed off that the guy next to me was 24 and running circles around me—I wasn't going to let *that* happen." He rose to the challenge, and over the years, started to attract attention of his own. After *Edible Manhattan* profiled him with a four-page spread, Pedro realized the moment would never be better to launch his own project. ("If you just stick around long enough, people notice you," he quips.)

Like many Brooklyn bars, his aim was to create a neighborhood spot with character—comfortable and social, with better cocktails than most; "Why *can't* your local bar have really good drinks?" he says. "How do we take everything I've learned about cocktails, and keep that, but make the whole experience more approachable?"

He landed in Prospect Heights, part of a section of Brooklyn he refers to as his "spiritual homeland." "This area is so fantastic for people; it's not just culturally diverse, it's economically diverse," he says. "A bar, to me, should be like the subway, where people talk to each other—they're random meeting places, community centers. If the stranger sitting next to you is a lot like you, it's a limited experience, but if it's someone completely different, and you find a way to relate to each other—that's so valuable."

❝ Why *can't* your local bar have really good drinks? How do we take everything I've learned about cocktails, and keep that, but make the whole experience more approachable? ❞
—Del Pedro, Tooker Alley

Pedro sees his mixology style as primarily rooted in the classics, with intelligent riffs on the Negroni, the daiquiri, the Manhattan, and others—though he does occasionally detour into the more esoteric. "To me, it's about following your muse, whether it's a crazy idea, or a new spirit you come across . . . but then you really do have to rely on your judgement. Is it weird but good, or do you just like it *because* it's weird?"

Tooker Alley's physical menu explodes with energy, a binder with cocktail descriptions in pages between poems, drinking songs, sketches drawn by customers, a glossary of early-20th-century hobo symbology. ("Hobo culture is something I'm really fascinated with; there's a core element of freedom that I really admire.")

The bar's namesake Tooker Alley, in Chicago, was the address of the Bohemian "Dill Pickle Club," an early-20th-century venue known for its free thinking and openmindedness. "It was a bar and a debate club, a counterculture hub— there was all sorts of social alchemy there. It's a super creative place."

❝ That's what you can do in a place of your own—you can take things you love, and try to expand them . . . in a way people can enjoy and relate to. ❞
—Del Pedro, Tooker Alley

At Brooklyn's own Tooker Alley, there is a sense of living, untamed creativity that's palpable. "There's something a little *Alice in Wonderland*, 'down the rabbit hole' about it," admits Pedro. "But that's what you can do in a place of your own—you can take things you love, and try to expand them and generalize them in a way people can enjoy and relate to.

"A guy said, 'This menu's crazy!' and my response was, 'Not to me.'"

COCKTAIL RECIPES

Crown Heights Negroni (p. 219)
Manhattanite (p. 107)
Haymaker's Punch (p. 98)
Rum, Sodomy, and the Lash (p. 141)
Woody Guthrie (p. 130)
Huascar Daiquiri (p. 148)

TIA MIA

Ivy Mix, Leyenda

"I've been putting mezcal floats on my Mai Tais for years, and people love them," says Ivy Mix. It adds a smoky punch to the tiki classic. While admittedly extravagant, an orchid perched on the crushed ice makes a showstopper garnish.

1 oz/30 mL Appleton Reserve rum
1 oz/30 mL Del Maguey Vida mezcal
½ oz/15 mL Orgeat Works toasted almond orgeat
½ oz/15 mL Pierre Ferrand orange Curaçao
¾ oz/20 mL lime juice
¼ oz/10 mL simple syrup

Combine all the ingredients in a rocks glass with crushed ice. Garnish with an orchid, mint sprig, and lime wheel.

MAI TAI

Here's a drink so long disabused that many bartenders couldn't tell you what's really supposed to be in it. So let's head back to Trader Vic's original recipe: good Jamaican rum, orgeat, Curaçao, and lime.

1½ oz/45 mL Appleton Estate Signature Blend Jamaican rum
1 oz/30 mL lime juice
½ oz/15 mL orgeat
½ oz/15 mL Curaçao
1 dash Angostura bitters

Combine all the ingredients in a cocktail shaker with ice. Shake until well chilled and strain into a rocks glass with fresh ice, or crushed ice if available. Garnish with mint and a cherry.

100-YEAR-OLD CIGAR

Maks Pazuniak, Jupiter Disco

Illustrating how versatile rum can be, this stirred drink builds from a base of much-lauded Guatemalan rum Ron Zacapa 23, with Cynar and Benedictine bringing in herbal-bitter notes and a sparing dose of Laphroaig, a powerful smokiness. Once you taste the drink, the name is right on.

1¾ oz/50 mL Ron Zacapa 23 rum
½ oz/15 mL Cynar
½ oz/15 mL Benedictine
¼ oz/10 mL Laphroaig Scotch whisky
1 dash Angostura bitters

Combine all the ingredients in a mixing glass with ice. Stir until well chilled. Rinse a chilled coupe with absinthe. Strain into the coupe.

BELAFONTE

Tom Dixon, Roberta's

Rather than rely on one of the many coconut rums on the market—many of which, candidly, smell and taste like sunscreen—Tom Dixon infuses his own, for a shaken drink brightened by a vinegar-based strawberry shrub.

1 oz/30 mL coconut-infused white rum (recipe p. 267)
1 oz/30 mL Sailor Jerry spiced rum
½ oz/15 mL Cocchi Americano
½ oz/15 mL strawberry shrub (recipe p. 282)
½ oz/15 mL lemon juice
4 dashes Angostura bitters
Club soda

Combine all the ingredients in a cocktail shaker with ice. Shake until well chilled and double-strain into a Collins glass with fresh ice. Top with club soda. Garnish with a sprig of mint.

Tia Mia, Leyenda

TRY IT WITH
RUM

Rum often gets pigeonholed into the "sweet and tropical" category, which is a shame, as it's one of the most diverse spirits out there. Barrel-aged rums can play well in cocktails we normally associate with whiskey, including the Old Fashioned and Manhattan, whereas white rums can swap in for many gin classics, such as the Ron Collins (extremely popular in Cuba) or, more surprising still, a rum martini.

RUM MANHATTAN

2 oz/60 mL Bacardi 8 rum
1 oz/30 mL Carpano Antica Formula sweet vermouth
1 dash Angostura bitters

Combine all the ingredients in a mixing glass with ice. Stir until well chilled and strain into a chilled coupe. Garnish with an orange twist and a brandied cherry.

WHITE RUM MARTINI

Use a high-quality white rum with weight and body to pull off this stirred drink.

2 oz/60 mL Brugal Extra Dry rum
1 oz/30 mL Dolin dry vermouth
3 dashes orange bitters

Combine all the ingredients in a mixing glass with several cracked ice cubes. Stir until well chilled and strain into a chilled coupe. Garnish with a lemon twist.

RON COLLINS

2 oz/60 mL white rum
1 oz/30 mL lemon juice
¾ oz/20 mL simple syrup
2 oz/60 mL club soda

Combine the first three ingredients in a cocktail shaker with ice. Shake until well chilled and strain into a Collins glass with fresh ice. Top with the club soda. Garnish with a lemon wheel.

RUM OLD FASHIONED

2 oz/60 mL Diplomático Reserva rum
¼ oz/10 mL demerara syrup (1:1)
2 dashes Angostura bitters
2 dashes orange bitters

Combine all the ingredients in a mixing glass with several cracked ice cubes. Stir until well chilled and strain into a rocks glass with one large ice cube. Garnish with an expressed orange peel.

TRINIDAD OLD-FASHIONED

TOBY CECCHINI, LONG ISLAND BAR

Toby Cecchini created this Old Fashioned specifically to highlight Plantation Trinidad 2001 rum. "It's super-simple; I stripped it all down because I wanted to emphasize how whiskey-like this one rum is," he says. The sweetener is a pure reduced syrup of pressed apple cider from Wood's Cider Mill in Springfield, Vermont.

2 oz/60 mL Plantation Trinidad 2001 rum
½ tsp Willis Wood Boiled cider
3 dashes St. Elizabeth's allspice dram

In a mixing glass filled with ice, stir all the ingredients together until well chilled. Strain into a double old fashioned glass with one large ice cube. Garnish with twists of both orange and lemon.

FREE FALL
Grand Ferry Tavern

Rum is a natural partner to warm spices, so allspice dram is an ideal match for this autumnal cocktail.

1¼ oz/40 mL Denizen Merchant's
  Reserve rum
¾ oz/20 mL Dolin Rouge sweet vermouth
½ oz/15 mL apple cider
¼ oz/10 mL allspice dram
¼ oz/10 mL lemon juice

Combine all the ingredients in a cocktail shaker with ice. Shake until well chilled and strain into a double rocks glass with fresh ice.

Free Fall, Grand Ferry Tavern

RUM, SODOMY, AND THE LASH
Del Pedro, Tooker Alley

Winston Churchill is said to have said that "The only traditions of the Royal Navy are rum, sodomy, and the lash"—which makes for a cheeky cocktail name if ever there were one. Del Pedro's cocktail plays off the tropical rum-lime-coconut template with a spirit-forward stirred drink in which this aged Venezuelan rum takes center stage, the other flavors accents in the background.

1¾ oz/50 mL Santa Teresa 1796 rum
¼ oz/10 mL Lustau Don Nuño oloroso sherry
½ oz/15 mL Kalani coconut liqueur
¼ tsp lime syrup (recipe p. 272)

In a double old fashioned glass, stir all the ingredients over two cubes of ice. Add two fresh cubes on top. Garnish with freshly grated nutmeg.

RUM COUGAR MELONCAMP
Rob Krueger, Extra Fancy

Rum can pair with fruit flavors beyond the tropical, as in this shaken drink with melon, lime, and ginger. Krueger uses puree from the French producer Boiron, but notes that you can make it at home by pureeing ripe cantaloupe in a blender, straining, and then adding sugar to taste. Their ginger syrup, unlike many that use fresh ginger, is Pickett's medium spicy ginger beer syrup, cut 1:1 with simple syrup.

1¾ oz/50 mL Caña Brava rum
1 oz/30 mL melon puree
¾ oz/20 mL lime juice
½ oz/15 mL ginger syrup
¼ oz/10 mL Aperol

Combine all the ingredients in a cocktail shaker with ice. Shake until well chilled and strain into a coupe. Garnish with a cucumber coin.

COCKTAIL RECIPES

LONG ISLAND BAR

Veteran barman stumbles upon untouched mid-century corner bar and restaurant, painstakingly restores the space and makes it his own. It's a bartender's fantasy, all but a fairy tale. Yet it came true for Toby Cecchini and Joel Tompkins—though not in any kind of tidy way.

Long Island Bar, on a western stretch of Atlantic Avenue not far from the water, is now a thriving bar and restaurant, but its owners' path was a circuitous one. By 2008, Toby Cecchini was well known as the owner of the popular Manhattan bar Passerby—and for having invented the Cosmopolitan decades before, a point of grudging pride he refers to as his "albatross." (More on that, p. 76.) But after Passerby closed, he spent years pursuing projects that, thanks to the "mishaps and foibles of New York real estate," fell apart in their final stages.

> **This is a tavern, with good but simple food, and good but simple drinks.**
>
> —*Toby Cecchini, Long Island Bar*

In the interim, he walked by Long Island Restaurant & Bar in his own Brooklyn neighborhood every day—a time capsule of Art Deco restaurant space that, according to Cecchini, industry heavyweights up to and including Danny Meyer and Mario Batali had tried to get their hands on, with no success. "Everyone knew the story of that space—it was owned by some crazy Spanish woman who wouldn't talk to anyone, while just sitting there like an absolute gem."

A neighborhood friend, who owned a men's store and gallery on that corner, knew that Cecchini was looking to open a bar; one day he ventured, "What about the Long Island Restaurant across the street?" Cecchini's response was disbelief; wasn't the owner an old recluse? Didn't she turn down everyone who inquired into the space? "Well, not really. That's my grandmother."

In quick succession, Cecchini saw the space, got the nod of approval from said grandmother, Emma Sullivan—who is now in her mid-nineties, and still lives across the street—and he and Tompkins signed a lease. "I kept thinking, *This is a mirage. This is never going to happen.*" Yet it did.

Then commenced the arduous task of preserving as much as possible, while having to strip ceilings back to the 1860s, rework hopeless electrical wiring, and generally update a building that hadn't been touched in decades. "We went to the Formica wholesaler, and this color, 'Irish Moss'—they discontinued it in 1974." But the upsides were tremendous. "This bar is solid mahogany; you can't get solid mahogany anymore." When Sullivan and her two cousins walked into the restaurant for the first time after renovations were complete, all three burst into tears. "They're three women who spent 56 years in this space, every day," says Cecchini—overwhelmed by its resurrection.

And the bar itself? Cecchini believes that in any establishment, "the space will tell you what it is," and it did: "This is a tavern, with good but simple food, and good but simple drinks." It's well suited to the cocktail style of a man who calls himself a "super-classicist."

Though he mines the canon, Cecchini's cocktails are hardly by the book; his style emerges in nuance. Thus a Boulevardier that splits the rye base and the vermouth; an Old Fashioned designed to showcase the whiskey-like character of one particular rum; a house gimlet with a compelling lime-ginger cordial. "I like abbreviated lists," he says. "It tells people, *here are a few things we can do.*" Obviously it isn't all.

"Everybody at this bar is a super-veteran. Everyone can make whatever you want."

Leyenda

CACHAÇA

The national spirit of Brazil, sugar-based cachaça could be called a rum, though it differs from most rums in that it's distilled from fermented sugar cane juice, rather than molasses. (And because Brazil is very protective of the cachaça designation, to mark their product as something distinctive.) While much of the country's cachaça is mass-produced and more than a little harsh, several high-quality brands have come into the U.S. market in recent years, with Avuá cachaça in particular making waves in the mixology world; others include Leblon and Yaguara.

SHADOW BOXER
Ivy Mix, Leyenda

Ivy Mix features the artisanal cachaça Yaguara in this brilliant red, not-quite-a-Negroni with apricot eau-de-vie and grapefruit liqueur.

1½ oz/45 mL Yaguara cachaça
¾ oz/20 mL Campari
¾ oz/20 mL Dolin dry vermouth
¼ oz/10 mL Blume apricot eau-de-vie
¼ oz/10 mL Giffard pamplemousse

Combine all the ingredients in a mixing glass with ice. Stir until well chilled and strain into a coupe. Garnish with an orange twist.

CAIPIRINHA

The national drink of Brazil, and by far the most popular way to drink cachaça, the caipirinha is a simple, rustic cocktail with just lime, sugar, cachaça, and often Angostura bitters. Traditionally the drink is built in a rocks glass, crushing the limes before adding sugar and spirit, then given a brief stir; for more of a "cocktail bar" method, use simple syrup, and give it a quick shake, helping to integrate the flavors.

2 oz/60 mL cachaça
1 lime, halved, each half then quartered
¾ oz/20 mL simple syrup
1 dash Angostura bitters

Add the lime and simple syrup to the bottom of a cocktail shaker and muddle hard. Add the cachaça and ice, and give several strong back-and-forth shakes. Pour the drink (ice, limes, and all) into a rocks glass, and add a dash of bitters.

·3 AWESOME· HIGHBALLS

Liquor plus soda—could anything be simpler? Highballs—by definition, just a spirit plus a mixer—are the easiest cocktails in the book. Yet you'll find them much improved if made with a bartender's eye toward detail. Pay attention to proportions and garnish and you'll have a drink that's as professional as it is dead simple.

CUBA LIBRE

2 oz/60 mL white rum
4 oz/120 mL Coca-Cola

In a Collins glass with ice, stir together the rum and Coke. Squeeze in a lime wedge.

DARK AND STORMY

2 oz/60 mL Gosling's Black Seal rum
4 oz/120 mL Gosling's ginger beer

In a Collins glass with ice, stir together rum and ginger beer. Squeeze in a lime wedge.

EXTRA-GINGER DARK AND STORMY

2 oz/60 mL Gosling's Black Seal rum
1 oz/30 mL lime juice
¾ oz/20 mL ginger syrup (recipe p. 273)
2 oz/60 mL club soda

Combine the first three ingredients in a cocktail shaker with ice. Shake until well chilled and strain into a Collins glass with fresh ice. Top with club soda and garnish with a lime wedge.

GINGER CAIPIRINHA

Like a margarita or daiquiri, the caipirinha takes well to experimentation; fresh ginger syrup is a great match.

2 oz/60 mL cachaça
1 lime, halved, each half then quartered
¾ oz/20 mL ginger syrup (recipe p. 273)
1 dash Angostura bitters

Add the lime and simple syrup to the bottom of a cocktail shaker and muddle hard. Add the cachaça and ice, and give several strong back-and-forth shakes. Pour the drink (ice, limes, and all) into a rocks glass, and add a dash of bitters.

MAIDEN NAME

Ivy Mix, Leyenda

Cachaça steps in for Caribbean rum in Ivy Mix's creamy blended drink that plays with tiki flavors.

2 oz/60 mL Avua cachaça
½ oz/15 mL coconut milk
½ oz/15 mL Coco Lopez
¾ oz/20 mL vanilla syrup (recipe p. 272)
½ oz/15 mL lime juice
½ oz/15 mL cinnamon syrup (recipe p. 270)
¼ oz/10 mL passion fruit puree

Add all the ingredients to a blender with ice and blend. Serve in a tiki mug, garnished with freshly grated nutmeg and pineapple leaves.

6 TAKES ON THE DAIQUIRI

Most drinkers will hear "daiquiri" and think "frozen." But a daiquiri is a true classic, as essential to the canon as Manhattans and martinis—and a lot simpler than you might think. Rum, sugar, and fresh lime juice: That's all a true daiquiri entails.

"We as a cocktail culture are still recovering from the long-abused daiquiri," says Ian Hardie of Huckleberry Bar. "After fighting through the land of frozen drinks and Rose's lime juice, the daiquiri is making its way back." And as Hardie notes, it's exciting to see someone try a "real" daiquiri for the first time.

Try out a classic daiquiri in all its tart, simple glory before moving on to other renditions.

DAIQUIRI
TONIA GUFFEY

"One of the most perfect cocktails on earth, albeit highly underrated, is the daiquiri," says Guffey. "I like Banks 5 Island rum because it has a lot of depth; or for a cleaner, crisper taste I like El Dorado 3 Year."

2 oz/60 mL white rum
1 oz/30 mL lime juice
¾ oz/20 mL simple syrup

Combine all the ingredients in a cocktail shaker with ice. Shake until well chilled and strain into a coupe. Garnish with a thin lime wheel.

BASIL DAIQUIRI

The standard daiquiri is a canvas that takes well to additional flavors. Adding a few basil leaves takes the drink in a fragrant, herbal direction. There's no need to muddle the basil here; the good shaking it gets with ice will express its flavors just fine.

2 oz/60 mL white rum
1 oz/30 mL lime juice
¾ oz/20 mL simple syrup
5 basil leaves

Combine all the ingredients in a cocktail shaker with ice. Shake until well chilled and double strain into a coupe. Garnish with a large basil leaf, gently slapping it against your hand before placing it atop the drink.

HUASCAR DAIQUIRI
DEL PEDRO, TOOKER ALLEY

"This was created on the fly at 3:00 a.m. for a customer who had run me out of rum drinks," says Del Pedro. A float of dark, molasses-like Blackstrap rum doubles as a garnish.

2 oz/60 mL Flor de Caña 4 Year
¾ oz/20 mL lime juice
¾ oz/20 mL simple syrup
½ oz/15 mL Cruzan Blackstrap rum

Combine the first three ingredients in a cocktail shaker with ice. Shake until well chilled and strain into a coupe. Float the Blackstrap rum on top.

HEMINGWAY DAIQUIRI

It's said that this cocktail was invented at Havana's famed El Floridita bar for Ernest Hemingway himself, who could make his way through a dozen in a day. (Like all Hemingway drinking stories, this one should be greeted with a bit of skepticism.) Regardless, it's a beautifully sophisticated drink, with grapefruit in addition to lime and with the cherry liqueur maraschino taking the sweet role.

2 oz/60 mL white rum
¾ oz/20 mL grapefruit juice
½ oz/15 mL lime juice
¼ oz/10 mL Luxardo maraschino liqueur

Combine all the ingredients in a cocktail shaker with ice. Shake until well chilled and strain into a coupe. Garnish with a lime wheel.

GUERRA FRÍA (COLD WAR)
TORREY BELL-EDWARDS, WILLOW

A take on a Hemingway daiquiri, the Guerra Fría (which translates to "cold war") uses bitters and mint to round out the sweet-sour profile.

1½ oz/45 mL white rum
¾ oz/20 mL lime juice
¼ oz/10 mL Luxardo maraschino liqueur
¼ oz/10 mL simple syrup
3 dashes grapefruit bitters
3 dashes Peychaud's bitters
Mint oil

Combine all the ingredients except the mint oil in a cocktail shaker with ice. Shake until well chilled and double-strain into a chilled rocks glass. Garnish with several drops of mint oil in uneven sizes.

MR. HOWELL
JUSTIN OLSEN, BEARDED LADY

From Prospect Heights cocktail bar Bearded Lady, this drink's clever addition of peated Scotch makes for a smoky, supple daiquiri.

1½ oz/45 mL rum (such as Flor de Caña 4 Year)
¾ oz/20 mL lime juice
½ oz/15 mL maple syrup
½ oz/15 mL peaty Islay whisky (Laphroaig, Lagavulin, etc.)

Combine all the ingredients in a cocktail shaker with ice. Shake until well chilled and double-strain into a coupe. Garnish with a lime wheel.

MARTINIQUAIS
THE RICHARDSON

Working within the daiquiri formula, this version uses a rhum agricole—a complex spirit distilled from sugar cane juice instead of molasses. Agricole brand Rhum J.M also reduces their pure cane juice and bottles it as a syrup, an intuitive partner for the rum itself.

2 oz/60 mL Rhum J.M Silver
½ oz/15 mL lime juice
½ oz/15 mL J.M Cane Sirop

Combine all the ingredients in a cocktail shaker with ice. Shake until well chilled and strain into a double rocks glass with fresh ice.

All spirits go through cycles of favor and disfavor. Rum, which many drinkers never gave a thought beyond the mojito, grew into a bartender obsession; vodka is less favored by mixologists at the moment, unless, perhaps, it's come back around—trends can change even month over month.

But few spirits were ever as maligned and misunderstood as tequila. Before the last decade, many of us only knew tequila as a shot, with salt and lime; or in margaritas laden with sour mix. (And many of us have blamed bad decisions in our college years on both.) Yet as bartenders have taken interest in well-made tequilas—and better bottles have made their way into the States—drinkers have had more opportunities than ever to appreciate the spirit as it should be appreciated.

Tequila itself is one corner of a spirit category called mezcal which, we should note, has two meanings. *Mezcal* as a category refers to any spirit distilled from fermented agave, so tequila qualifies (though it must meet additional regulations, in terms of the agave species and where it's grown, to be properly called *tequila*). Lesser-known spirits like bacanora and raicilla are *mezcales* as well.

But the "mezcal" you'll see on a cocktail list or in a liquor store? That refers to a more specific spirit (with its own set of regulations). The agave hearts for mezcal are generally roasted in an underground

TEQUILA, Mezcal, y Mas

earthen oven before they're crushed and the juice is fermented, which imparts a distinct smoky flavor that mezcal fans go nuts for. (So mezcal is a mezcal; tequila is a mezcal; but not all mezcals are tequilas. Got that?)

Like rum, the categories of tequila are quite distinct. Blanco (silver) tequila is unaged; *reposado*, or "rested," is barrel-aged between two months and one year; and añejo, between one and three years. (Extra-añejos, aged more than three years, do exist, though they're rare and expensive.)

Like whiskey, dark rums, and other aged spirits, tequila picks up more barrel character the longer it ages, and becomes smoother and richer. Bartenders will use blanco tequilas, or occasionally reposados, in most mixed drinks; where you see añejo in a cocktail, it'll play a role similar to whiskey, such as in an Old Fashioned.

And there's a dramatic range of flavors within any category. "As far as mixing goes," says Ivy Mix of Leyenda, which specializes in New World spirits, "tequila is delicious stuff; there are so many flavor profiles between highland and lowland tequilas. Highlands, like Siembra Azul, can be floral and citrusy, and make a great margarita; lowland tequilas like Fortaleza can be more peppery, robust, and intense."

CHAPTER 6

BA'SIK

Jay Zimmerman came up in the industry through managing a number of high-profile Manhattan bars—the bar programs at the eternally popular Standard Hotel and Ace Hotel among them—but when he opened Ba'sik in East Williamsburg, he wasn't gunning for a groundbreaking cocktail program. "I wasn't thinking about the New York nightlife scene. I was thinking about how it'd immediately affect East Williambsurg, how it'd affect this stop on this L train."

> ❝ I love my little corner of Brooklyn. And I've really grown to love this bar . . . ❞
>
> —Jay Zimmerman, Ba'sik

The result is a cozy but sophisticated bar—urbane with its concrete and reclaimed wood—where regulars reign. "People who live in this part of Williamsburg are really loyal to the neighborhood; they don't have this need to go into Manhattan all the time," he says. Including Zimmerman himself, who happens to live two doors away—an apartment he'd had long before looking at spaces. "When our crowd is 80% regulars, it's hard for me to just drop by anymore . . . I'm pumping mitts all the way around the bar."

As for cocktails, Zimmerman goes for intelligent, well-made crowd-pleasers, like the bourbon-ginger-mint Poppa's Pride and the chamomile-honey-vodka O.V.C. "I get influences from a lot of places, from tasting and trying new things, whether nationally, internationally, or even in New York." But he's not trying to push the boundary of cocktail culture; rather, to make drinks that people love, and remember, and come back for. "At the end of the day, I believe more in hospitality than I do in cocktails," he says. "I would so much rather give someone a drink that they want and order, not what *I* think they should be drinking."

"I love my little corner of Brooklyn. And I've really grown to love this bar," says Zimmerman, looking around Ba'sik's comfortable backyard. "I'll sit here and realize what we've built, and you know what? It's pretty great."

COCKTAIL RECIPES

O.V.C. (p. 66)
Poppa's Pride (p. 93)
Bright Hatchet (p. 157)
Triple Crown (p. 95)
Back Porch Punch (p. 164)
Death in the Afternoon (p. 253)

❝ I would so much rather give someone a drink that they want and order, not what I think they should be drinking. ❞
—*Jay Zimmerman, Ba'sik*

TEQUILA

ROSARITA
David Moo, Quarter Bar

Rosemary and egg white take this tequila cocktail away from the traditional margarita format, for a drink that's light, herbal, and almost delicate in its texture.

1½ oz/45 mL blanco tequila
¾ oz/20 mL lime juice
¾ oz/20 mL rosemary simple syrup
  (recipe p. 277)
½ oz/15 mL egg white

Combine all the ingredients in a cocktail shaker with ice. Shake until well chilled and strain into a coupe.

MAIN LAND
Achilles Heel

Tequila's vegetal elements play well with slightly savory ingredients, like the beet shrub used in this lively cocktail from Achilles Heel. The fresh fennel on top defines the drink; don't skip the garnish.

1¼ oz/40 mL blanco tequila
¾ oz/20 mL Cocchi Torino
½ oz/15 mL grapefruit juice
½ oz/15 mL beet shrub (recipe p. 283)
1 tsp lime juice

Combine all the ingredients in a cocktail shaker with ice. Shake until well chilled and double-strain into a coupe. Garnish with fresh fennel fronds.

Rosarita, Quarter Bar

HIKE IN THE DESERT
David Sheridan, Wheated

"One of our servers went to New Orleans and came back describing a drink with sage and Laphroaig," says David Sheridan, who uses those flavors in this gently smoky tequila cocktail; "I never was happy with the experiment with whisky but did find this one to be very pleasing."

2 oz/60 mL blanco tequila
1 oz/30 mL lime juice
¾ oz/20 mL agave syrup (2:1)
4 sage leaves
Laphroaig Islay 10 Year Scotch whisky

Rinse the inside of a coupe with Laphroaig, discarding excess, and set coupe aside. Lightly muddle the sage leaves in the bottom of a cocktail shaker. Add the remaining ingredients and ice and shake until well chilled. Double-strain into the prepared coupe, and garnish with a sage leaf.

HAPPY/SAD GIRL

Katherine Pangaro, No. 7

Fresh ginger syrup enlivens this tequila drink, balanced with lime and maraschino liqueur.

2 oz/60 mL blanco tequila
¾ oz/20 mL ginger syrup (recipe p. 273)
¾ oz/20 mL lime juice
½ oz/15 mL maraschino liqueur
Club soda

Combine all the ingredients except club soda in a cocktail shaker with ice. Shake until well chilled and strain into a rocks glass with fresh ice. Top with a splash of soda, and garnish with a lime wheel and/or candied ginger.

BRIGHT HATCHET

Jay Zimmerman, Ba'sik

Tequila and citrus are a very common pairing, but rather than using fresh juices, Jay Zimmerman changes up the format with grapefruit liqueur.

1¼ oz/40 mL Olmeca Altos reposado tequila
1 oz/30 mL Cocchi rosso vermouth
¾ oz/20 mL Combier pamplemousse rose
3 drops Bittercube orange bitters
2 drops rose water

Combine all the ingredients in a mixing glass with ice. Stir until well chilled and strain into a coupe. Garnish with a grapefruit twist.

TRY IT WITH TEQUILA

TEQUILA OLD FASHIONED

An Old Fashioned generally features whiskey, but the long barrel-aging of an añejo tequila gives it many of the same characteristics; agave syrup, as agave itself is the basis of tequila, is the ideal sweetener.

2 oz/60 mL añejo tequila
¼ oz/10 mL agave syrup (1:1)
2 dashes orange bitters
2 dashes Angostura bitters

Combine all the ingredients in a mixing glass with several cracked ice cubes. Stir until well chilled and strain into a rocks glass with one large ice cube. Garnish with one orange peel and one lime peel.

TEQUILA-GRONI

Gin is delicious in a Negroni; why not try its fellow clear spirit? The slight sharp bite and vegetal character of a good silver tequila pairs up nicely with bittersweet Campari.

1½ oz/45 mL blanco tequila
1 oz/30 mL Carpano Antica Formula sweet vermouth
1 oz/30 mL Campari

Combine all the ingredients in a mixing glass with several cracked ice cubes. Stir until well chilled and strain into a rocks glass with one large ice cube. Garnish with an expressed orange peel.

SIGNIFICANT OTHER
Tom Dixon, Roberta's

Another reflection of tequila's complexity, this shaken drink brings in elements both fruity (apricot liqueur) and vegetal (celery). Rather than muddle the celery, Dixon keeps the pieces intact for a shaken drink "that comes out really fresh and light."

2 oz/60 mL el Jimador blanco tequila
¾ oz/20 mL lime juice
½ oz/15 mL Rothmans apricot liqueur
½ oz/15 mL agave syrup (1:1)
8 small pieces chopped celery

Combine all the ingredients in a cocktail shaker with ice. Shake until well chilled and strain into a rocks glass with fresh ice. Garnish with a celery leaf.

MEZCAL

LITTLE ZEDDIE
Achilles Heel

Bittersweet and slightly citrusy, the Italian amaro CioCaro adds complexity and depth to this smoky mezcal drink.

1½ oz/45 mL Union mezcal
½ oz/15 mL CioCiaro amaro
½ oz/15 mL lime juice
5 dashes orange bitters

Combine all the ingredients in a cocktail shaker with ice. Shake until well chilled and double-strain into a coupe.

KING MEDICINE
Tonia Guffey, Dram

"Here's a spin on your classic margarita-style drink," says Tonia Guffey, "with rosemary and pineapple, which are really pretty together, but unexpected. Chartreuse reinforces the herbaceousness."

1 oz/30 mL Corralejo blanco tequila
½ oz/15 mL Del Maguey Vida mezcal
1 oz/30 mL pineapple juice
½ oz/15 mL green Chartreuse
½ oz/15 mL lime juice
¼ oz/10 mL simple syrup
2 dashes Hellfire bitters
Rosemary sprig

Combine the first seven ingredients and the bottom half of the rosemary sprig in a cocktail shaker with ice. Shake until well chilled and double-strain into a coupe. Garnish with the top half of the rosemary stalk.

OAXACA FLOCA FLAME
Mayfield

Smoke and spice are a compelling pairing here, with watermelon to keep those powerful flavors in check.

1½ oz/45 mL Fidencio mezcal
1 oz/30 mL watermelon juice
¾ oz/20 mL ancho simple syrup
  (recipe p. 273)
½ oz/15 mL lime juice

Combine all the ingredients in a cocktail shaker with ice. Shake until well chilled and double-strain into a coupe.

King Medicine, Dram

LEYENDA

"Some bartenders, their whole entry into the industry is, *I'm going to read this fancy cocktail book, and now I want to be a bartender,*" says Ivy Mix of today's mixology world. "Whereas I bartended in Guatemala for four years before I knew what a real cocktail was."

> ❝ I can be creative and bartend at the same time? It's the best of both worlds. ❞
>
> —Ivy Mix, Leyenda

During her time living and traveling in Latin America, Mix couldn't have been farther from New York's intense cocktail culture. But over her years there, she got to know the brand Ilegal mezcal—so-called because they would smuggle the spirit over borders; and when she moved to New York, her contacts tipped her off to a mezcal bar opening in Manhattan, called Mayahuel. She went after a bartending job—"though at the time I'd never made anything more complicated than a mojito"—and ended up as a cocktail waitress. Though she wasn't behind the bar, Mayahuel was her first real look into the NYC mixology world. "Mayahuel where I really *got* it. Before, I had no idea what cocktails could be." It was a revelation: "I can be creative *and* bartend at the same time? It's the best of both worlds."

Fort Defiance in Red Hook gave Mix her first cocktail bartending gig, followed by Clover Club, where she worked under industry superstar Julie Reiner for years. "Even at Clover—

which is more of a gin and whiskey bar—all my cocktails always had mezcal in them, or tequila, or pisco. Those are the spirits I work with."

So when a space across the street from Clover Club opened up—and Reiner wanted to open a Latin American bar and restaurant—Mix was the clear favorite. Her menu at Leyenda encompasses all manner of Latin spirits, from Central American rums to Mexican agave spirits to Peruvian pisco and Brazilian cachaça.

Mix has been pleasantly surprised by how many people are open to tequila, pisco, and rum cocktails, and how many even come in with knowledge of their own. "I've had more people coming in asking, 'What types of mezcal do you have?' rather than asking, 'What's mezcal?'"—showing just how far the spirits world has come.

COCKTAIL RECIPES

Tía Mía (p. 138)
Buena Onda (p. 192)
Shadow Boxer (p. 146)
Maiden Name (p. 147)
Sonámbula (p. 173)

"All my cocktails always had mezcal in them, or tequila, or pisco. Those are the spirits I work with."

—Ivy Mix, Leyenda

THE HIDDEN HAND

Jonny Sela, Sisters

While fresh fruits are a staple of mixology, an increasing number of high-end fruit liqueurs are hitting the market. "They open up a whole new arena of flavor experimentation," says Jonny Sela, who uses Giffard's Banane du Brésil to incorporate banana flavors in with smoky, fruity, and herbal elements.

1½ oz/45 mL Del Maguey Vida mezcal
½ oz/15 mL Sapins liqueur
½ oz/15 mL Giffard Banane du Brésil
¼ oz/10 mL crème de cacao
¾ oz/20 mL lemon juice
¾ oz/20 mL pineapple juice

Combine all the ingredients in a cocktail shaker with ice. Shake until well chilled and double-strain into a rocks glass with fresh ice. Garnish with a sprinkle of cocoa powder and an orange twist.

KING'S PEACH

Mayfield

Mezcal's smokiness can be paired with any number of flavors, as in this stirred cocktail that brings in peach liqueur and the almond-clove-lime notes of velvet falernum as faint supporting notes to an excellent spirit.

2¼ oz/70 mL Fidencio mezcal
¼ oz/10 mL velvet falernum
¼ oz/10 mL crème de pêche
1 dash mole bitters

Combine all the ingredients in a mixing glass with ice. Stir until well chilled and strain into a rocks glass with fresh ice. Garnish with a lemon twist.

BACK PORCH PUNCH

Jay Zimmerman, Ba'sik

Building from the template of a margarita, Jay Zimmerman adds an unexpected twist—Shiner's Ruby Redbird Radler, a lager with ruby red grapefruit juice and a hint of ginger.

1½ oz/45 mL Del Maguey Vida mezcal
¾ oz/20 mL lime juice
½ oz/15 mL Luxardo Triplum orange liqueur
½ oz/15 mL simple syrup
Shiner Ruby Redbird Radler

Combine all the ingredients except the Radler in a cocktail shaker with ice. Shake until well chilled and strain into a Collins glass with fresh ice. Top with about 3 oz/90 mL of Radler and garnish with a half-wheel of grapefruit.

PILAR

The Narrows

At The Narrows, "we love simplicity in cocktails, and this is a great example of that ethos at play." They note that, while bright red Cappelletti might cosmetically resemble Campari (more on these ingredients, p. 215), they're dramatically different: Don't be tempted to substitute!

1½ oz/45 mL El Buho mezcal
1 oz/30 mL Cocchi Americano
½ oz/15 mL Cappelletti

Combine all the ingredients in a mixing glass with ice. Stir until well chilled and strain into a chilled coupe. Garnish with an orange twist.

EL DIABLO RUN

Kate O'Connor Morris, Rose's

Like the Paloma, an easy-drinking tequila sipper; unlike the Paloma, it pairs tequila with spicy ginger beer, lifted with a bit of lime.

1½ oz/45 mL **Espolón tequila blanco**
¼ oz/10 mL **El Dorado 5 Year rum**
¼ oz/10 mL **lime juice**
Blenheim ginger ale
  (or another spicy brand)

Combine the first three ingredients in a Collins glass with ice. Squeeze in an orange slice. Top with ginger ale. Garnish with a lime wedge.

Mezcals and barware, Leyenda

THE PALOMA

Everyone knows the margarita, but what's the most popular drink in Mexico itself? (Besides a cold *cerveza*, that is?) The Paloma. In its simplest form, it's a mix of grapefruit soda (like Jarritos or Squirt) and tequila, served tall over ice. In this version, real grapefruit and lime give you a more vibrant, citrusy drink. (Adjust the simple syrup in this drink to taste; depending on how sweet your grapefruit juice is, you may need more or less.)

2 oz/60 mL **blanco tequila**
1 oz/30 mL **grapefruit juice**
½ oz/15 mL **lime juice**
½ oz/15 mL **simple syrup**
Club soda

If you wish, salt the rim of a Collins glass. Fill the glass with ice, the tequila, the simple syrup, and the juices. Stir briefly and top with club soda.

SPRING PIGEON
CHILO'S

This take on the Paloma adds a splash of Pacífico beer for a drink that's a bit unusual but just as refreshing. They recommend rimming the glass in Tajín, a popular Mexican seasoning powder.

1½ oz/45 mL **Hornitos blanco tequila**
½ oz/15 mL **lime juice**
Jarritos grapefruit soda
Pacífico beer

In a Collins glass with ice, combine the tequila and lime juice. Fill with grapefruit soda until two fingers from the top, then top with a splash of beer. Garnish with a grapefruit twist.

NIGHT SHIFT
The Richardson

Tequila-grapefruit-Campari is a combination that gets a lot of play; at The Richardson, it's tweaked with mezcal as the base spirit and a warm-spice note from cinnamon syrup.

1¼ oz/40 mL Las Hormigas mezcal
1 oz/30 mL grapefruit juice
½ oz/15 mL Campari
¼ oz/10 mL cinnamon syrup (recipe p. 270)

Combine all the ingredients in a cocktail shaker with ice. Shake until well chilled and strain into a double rocks glass with fresh ice. Garnish with an orange twist.

ERIKA MARIE
Nathan Ricke, Exley

Mezcal can have a lighter side, as in this shaken drink with grapefruit liqueur, fresh lime, and orangey Aperol, interpreting the margarita model through a different perspective.
A salt-pepper rim serves as a riff on the margarita standard.

1 oz/30 mL mezcal
¾ oz/20 mL Aperol
¾ oz/20 mL Combier pamplemousse rose
¾ oz/20 mL lime juice
¼ cup/ 60 g Kosher salt
2 tbsp/30 g Freshly ground black pepper

Make a mix of the pepper and kosher salt. Moisten the rim of a chilled coupe with a lime wedge and dip in the salt and pepper mix; set the coupe aside. Combine the first four ingredients in a cocktail shaker with ice. Shake until well chilled and double-strain into the coupe.

ON DRINKING ALONE

There's a pretty strong connotation to "drinking alone" in our culture—but heading to a bar by yourself isn't only for depressives and alcoholics. In fact, one of the best ways to get to know a bartender is to fly solo on a reasonably quiet night. "I'm always happy when people come in alone," says Ivy Mix of Leyenda.

> " I'm always happy when people come in alone ... I think it's the sign of a good bar, that they're comfortable enough to do so. "
>
> —Ivy Mix, Leyenda

"I think it's the sign of a good bar, that they're comfortable enough to do so." And engaging with those curious customers is many bartenders' favorite part of the job. A seat at the bar is always best if you're fascinated by the action. "I love it when people sit at the bar and they feel comfortable enough to ask questions," says Joel Lee Kulp of The Richardson and Grand Ferry Tavern. "The bar's the best place to do it: *I've never tasted this before, what's it like, what can you do with it?* I don't see the bartender as the keeper of all these secrets that nobody should know. The bartender is the expert who's there for you."

SMOKING JACKET
Darren Grenia, Dear Bushwick

Again we see smoke (mezcal) and spice (an original chile-stout reduction), with lime and ginger to help integrate these powerful flavors.

2 oz/60 mL El Peletón de la Muerte mezcal
¾ oz/20 mL lime juice
½ oz/15 mL ginger syrup (recipe p. 273)
¼ oz/10 mL chile-stout reduction
   (recipe p. 283)
4 drops Bittermens Xocolatl mole bitters

Combine all the ingredients in a cocktail shaker with ice. Shake until well chilled and strain into a coupe. Garnish with a lime twist.

LAUGHING DAISY
Jenna Meade, The Vanderbilt

While some agave drinks are all about the chiles—more on that to come—other drinks just let a bit of heat lurk around the edges, like this cucumber-mezcal cocktail with spicy Hellfire bitters.

1½ oz/45 mL Del Maguey Vida mezcal
1 oz/30 mL lime juice
½ oz/15 mL yellow Chartreuse
¼ oz/10 mL honey syrup (1:1)
1-inch/25-mm segment of cucumber
4 to 5 drops Hellfire bitters

Rim half a rocks glass with a mix of cayenne and salt. Fill the glass with ice. In the bottom of a cocktail shaker, muddle the cucumber. Add the remaining ingredients and ice and shake until well chilled. Double-strain into the glass.

Smoking Jacket, Dear Bushwick

MARGARITAS

The margarita isn't just a drink; it's a category. Even mediocre Mexican restaurants are likely to offer you a strawberry or mango margarita alongside their standard lime. But that's not what we're talking about here. When made correctly, with fresh juice and high-quality spirits, the margarita is a respected drink in the sour tradition, and tequila and lime is a combination to play around with endlessly.

CLASSIC MARGARITA

It's hard to argue with this rendition on the classic. As always, fresh juice is imperative, and using a higher-quality orange liqueur, whether Cointreau or Combier, will be a huge improvement on cheaper triple secs.

2 oz/60 mL blanco tequila
1 oz/30 mL lime juice
1 oz/30 mL orange liqueur

Combine all the ingredients in a cocktail shaker with ice. Shake until well chilled and strain into a rocks glass with fresh ice. Garnish with a lime wheel.

COCKTAIL RECIPES

HOTEL DELMANO

In 2006, Williamsburg was still largely a land of whiskey-and-beer bars—as Zeb Stewart and Alyssa Abeyta knew well, as co-owners of the still-iconic Union Pool, which fit that mold itself. "But we aged out of our own bar," says Abeyta. "There was no place for adults to drink and have a conversation."

That's what inspired them to open Hotel Delmano, one of the first sophisticated cocktail bars in a neighborhood that now has dozens. "We wanted to make it seem like we discovered an old, beautiful bar and reopened it," says Stewart. "We were influenced heavily by Havana, that sort of decomposed architecture, and Argentina; we were all in love with Argentina at that time." Of course, it takes effort to fashion a space in controlled "decay," and both Stewart and co-owner Michael Smart were instrumental in crafting it.

If its mahogany-and-marble, carefully worn aesthetic seems familiar in cocktail bars today, that's in large part thanks to Delmano. And their opening coincided with a real moment in cocktail culture, which their current but classically-inspired cocktail program fit right into. "We were a little surprised by the success of it, honestly!" says Stewart. "We thought it might be five or six old-timers; we were stunned when there was a line out the door and we couldn't seat everyone."

Though their cocktail list earned early fans, Stewart and Abeyta agreed that that wasn't all they wanted. "Instead of an ode to the cocktail," says Abeyta, "it was more about people and experience." While keeping up with the craft cocktail world, and as prone to getting excited about sherry or mezcals as anyone out there, the Delmano team didn't want to push their bar too far in a mixology-geek direction. "There should be some kind of balance between your nerdy obsession and the customers," according to Stewart. "You're trying to find a place in between, when customers are learning without being talked down to, but bartenders still enjoy making the drinks. Cocktails are supposed to be delicious and fun and you should be able to throw them back."

> ❛❛ Cocktails are supposed to be delicious and fun and you should be able to throw them back. ❜❜ —*Zeb Stewart, Hotel Delmano*

Delmano hit Williamsburg and the cocktail world at the right moment to thrive, but its owners don't see it as a trendy bar in the least. "It feels timeless to me," says Abeyta. "I think in twenty years, you could walk in and it would feel much the same."

> **It feels timeless to me...I think in twenty years, you could walk in and it would feel much the same.**
> —*Alyssa Abeyta, Hotel Delmano*

TOMMY'S MARGARITA

Some bartenders prefer an alternate version of the standard margarita, popularized by Julio Bermejo, co-owner of Tommy's Mexican Restaurant in San Francisco—thus the name. A Tommy's leaves the orange liqueur behind, instead gently sweetening with agave (the base of tequila itself). A little crisper and cleaner than the classic. Try both and see which you prefer.

2 oz/60 mL blanco tequila
1 oz/30 mL lime juice
½ oz/15 mL agave syrup (1:1)

Combine all the ingredients in a cocktail shaker with ice. Shake until well chilled and strain into a rocks glass with fresh ice. Garnish with a lime wheel.

MARGARITA DE PEPINO
Gran Electrica

"Cucumber pairs exceptionally well with the herbal notes of the cilantro," says Tamer Hamawi, co-owner of Gran Electrica," which makes for a much more interesting alternative to just plain old simple syrup."

1½ oz/45 mL Pueblo Viejo blanco tequila
½ oz/15 mL Combier triple sec
1 oz/30 mL lime juice
1 oz/30 mL cucumber juice
½ oz/15 mL cilantro syrup (recipe p. 280)

Combine all the ingredients in a cocktail shaker with ice. Shake until well chilled and strain into a rocks glass with fresh ice. Garnish with a cucumber slice.

JALAPEÑO MARGARITA

Spicy margaritas are tequila's latest breakout hit. One thin slice of jalapeño will give this drink a little tingle; three will get it to full-on spicy.

2 oz/60 mL blanco tequila
1 oz/30 mL lime juice
½ oz/15 mL agave syrup (1:1)
1 to 3 thin slices jalapeño pepper

In the bottom of a cocktail shaker, briefly muddle the jalapeño. Add all the other ingredients and ice. Shake until well chilled and strain into a rocks glass with fresh ice. Garnish with a lime wheel.

MEZCAL MARGARITA

If you're into smoky flavors, mezcal makes an excellent margarita as well, and can be a great entry point for those who aren't yet familiar with the spirit—what's less intimidating than a margarita?

2 oz/60 mL Fidencio mezcal
1 oz/30 mL lime juice
½ oz/15 mL agave syrup (1:1)

Combine all the ingredients in a cocktail shaker with ice. Shake until well chilled and strain into a coupe. Garnish with a lime wheel.

AN EASY TEQUILA PARTY DRINK

S uccessful cocktails require precision . . . usually. But when you're midway through a party, you're unlikely to break out the jigger and the Hawthorne strainer. It's always worth having a few "cocktail" ideas in your back pocket, and what's more party-friendly than tequila?

"Not fancy does not equal not delicious!" says Liz Stauber from The Narrows. "In a big cup with ice, pour in a couple glugs of blanco tequila, a glug of Campari, grapefruit soda, and a lime wedge. Done."

SPICY DRINKS

Margaritas with a kick of heat—generally from jalapeño, though recipes vary—are so commonplace now that cocktail bartenders hear them ordered even when they're *not* on a cocktail list. There's something addictive in a drink that leaves your tongue tingling; many bar-goers can't get enough. And more often than not, spicy drinks are tequila drinks. Why? Tequila's Mexican origins play a part, perhaps, as that cuisine makes use of so many chiles. But there's also a certain bite to blanco tequilas that a little heat helps to pick up.

SONÁMBULA
Ivy Mix, Leyenda

Chamomile tea, mellow and soothing, is an unexpected (but excellent) partner to jalapeño tequila in Ivy Mix's cocktail, whose name translates to "sleepwalker."

2 oz/60 mL jalapeño-infused tequila
  (recipe p. 268)
1 oz/30 mL lemon juice
¾ oz/20 mL chamomile syrup (recipe p. 280)
1 dash mole bitters
1 dash Peychaud's bitters

Combine all the ingredients in a cocktail shaker with ice. Shake until well chilled and strain into a coupe. Garnish with a lemon wheel.

Word, The Narrows

SAMPOGNA

Ian Hardie, Huckleberry Bar

Intensely spicy jalapeño-infused tequila takes center stage in this cocktail from Ian Hardie, with elderflower St-Germain and honey to tame the heat (if just a bit).

1½ oz/45 mL jalapeño-infused tequila (recipe p. 268)
1 oz/30 mL lemon juice
1 oz/30 mL honey syrup (2:1 hot water to honey)
½ oz/15 mL St-Germain

Combine all ingredients in a cocktail shaker with ice. Shake until well chilled and strain into a rocks glass with fresh ice. Garnish with a pickled jalapeño.

WORD

The Narrows

Based on a classic cocktail called the Last Word (recipe p. 57), this "Word" splits its base between jalapeño tequila and smoky, peaty Laphroaig—paired with chartreuse and maraschino, it's a bit of a head trip, but one worth taking.

½ oz/15 mL jalapeño-infused tequila (recipe p. 268)
½ oz/15 mL Laphroaig Scotch whisky
¾ oz/20 mL green Chartreuse
¾ oz/20 mL maraschino liqueur
¾ oz/20 mL lime juice
1 dash Angostura bitters

Combine all the ingredients in a cocktail shaker with ice. Shake until well chilled and strain into a coupe.

THE DEVIL'S GARDEN

Sam Anderson, Hotel Delmano

In one of Delmano's most popular drinks, chipotle peppers are a perfect match for smoky mezcal, evened out by lime and agave and given a complex, bitter note with Cynar.

1 oz/30 mL chipotle-infused mezcal (recipe p. 268)
1 oz/30 mL blanco tequila
¾ oz/20 mL lime juice
¾ oz/20 mL agave syrup (3 agave:1 water)
½ oz/15 mL Cynar
1 dash Angostura bitters

Combine all the ingredients in a cocktail shaker with ice and shake vigorously. Double-strain into a chilled cocktail coupe. Garnish with a fresh mint leaf.

Sampogna, Huckleberry Bar

BRANDY, in All Its Forms

Bourbon, gin, mezcal—all tend to grab attention on cocktail lists. Once-less-appreciated ingredients like sherry and rum have gained traction, too. Brandy? It doesn't really get the pulse going. To most modern drinkers, brandy sounds stuffy, a bit old-fashioned; isn't that what old British gentlemen sip in the library after dinner?

Well—yes. But it's far more than that. Brandy isn't a single spirit, but a huge category: Any spirit distilled from fruit is a brandy. So there's grape-based Cognac and its ilk, sure, but there's also apple brandy (the oldest American distillery, in fact, makes apple brandy), pear brandy, and others. Pisco, the national spirit of Peru and Chile, may not look like what we generally think of as "brandy," as it's a clear spirit, but it is an unaged grape brandy.

While it may not sound exciting to many bar enthusiasts, bartenders appreciate the diversity of the category, the history of each distinct spirit, and their many applications in cocktails.

177

THE DRINK

A nautically inspired bar amongst the dives of East Williamsburg, with a menu of historically inspired punches, a refurbished piano that invites impromptu performances, and traditions ranging from Pentecost parties (with mead and sword fighting) to apple festivals (with dozens of ciders and bluegrass music); it's hard to neatly sum up The Drink. But all its eccentricities, many as they are, evolved organically. "Most of the owners here were raised sailing, so the maritime theme is genuine," says co-owner Adam Collision. "The bar has become an extension of our personalities," according to his wife Nika Carlson; "There's a lot of weird stuff here because that's what we like."

The bar top is solid teak originally slated for sailboat construction; the bar's foot rail, a mast that never made its way to a boat. "Everyone in our families is a bit of a hoarder," says Carlson, "and everything in this bar has a story." (And there's plenty of it—Collision, charmingly, calls The Drink a "stuff-oriented bar.") Inquire into the curios and you may get more history than you'd bargained for.

As for the punch? "We're interested in history here," says Collision—and punch has a history dating back centuries. "Traditionally, punches were a combination of sugar, citrus, tea, and spirits, and that translates really well to modern cocktail culture." He and co-owner Frank Cisneros, "who always had a bowl of punch on the back bar at Prime Meats," were both enthusiasts, and when envisioning the bar, thought punch would suit The Drink and the atmosphere they sought to create: "It's a more communal, friendly way of drinking a cocktail."

Over the years, the team at The Drink has developed dozens of punch recipes with all manner of spirits, but their interests don't stop there. Cisneros developed a list of classics; and their crowd appreciates everything from $3 Narragansett beer to top-shelf whiskeys that approach $100 for a double pour.

"I think people want to be here because they're comfortable; we feel at home here and put ourselves into the bar," says Carlson. "We have regulars who call this place their second living room." And those regulars are themselves an eclectic bunch. "Our crowd is not definable," says manager Allie Zempel—clearly, the way they like it.

COCKTAIL RECIPES

The Old Gunwale (p. 182)

The Mutiny (p. 182)

Grace O'Malley (p. 182)

The Close Haul (p. 183)

La Guernica (p. 183)

> **"I think people want to be here because they're comfortable: *we* feel at home here and put ourselves into the bar."**
> —Nika Carlson, The Drink

5 PUNCHES FROM THE DRINK

THE OLD GUNWALE

10 oz/300 mL
Bernheim bourbon
8 oz/210 mL white
grapefruit juice
6 oz/180 mL chamomile syrup
(recipe p. 280)
5 oz/150 mL water
1 bar spoon Bittermens
New England Spiced
Cranberry bitters

Stir all the ingredients
together without ice,
then pour over ice in a
punch bowl. Garnish with
lemon wheels.

THE MUTINY

10 oz/300 mL Pueblo
Viejo tequila
10 oz/300 mL
watermelon juice
5 oz/150 mL lime juice
5 oz/150 mL simple syrup
1 bar spoon Brooklyn
Hemispherical Rhubarb bitters

Stir all the ingredients
together without ice, then
pour over ice in a punch
bowl. Garnish with a handful
of lightly bruised mint.

GRACE O'MALLEY

7½ oz/225 mL Teeling
Small Batch Irish whiskey
5 oz/150 mL Tuaca
5 oz/150 mL Barry's Tea
(one bag brewed for
6 minutes)
5 oz/150 mL green tea syrup
(recipe p. 280)
2½ oz/65 mL lemon juice
10 dashes Angostura bitters
10 dashes orange bitters

Stir all the ingredients
together without ice, then
pour over ice in a punch
bowl. Garnish with
lemon wheels.

The Mutiny, The Drink

THE CLOSE HAUL

10 oz/300 mL Damrak gin
7½ oz/225 mL cucumber juice
5 oz/150 mL lemon juice
5 oz/150 mL chamomile syrup
(recipe p. 280)
1 bar spoon Bittermens
Meyer Lemon bitters

Stir all the ingredients together without ice, then pour over ice in a punch bowl. Garnish with lemon wheels.

LA GUERNICA

10 oz Rittenhouse rye
4 oz/120 mL lemon juice
5 oz/150 mL lapsang
syrup (recipe p.278)
4 oz/120 mL hibiscus syrup
(recipe p.279)
1 oz/30 mL jalapeño tincture
(recipe p.269)
10 dashes Regan's orange bitters

Stir all the ingredients together without ice, then pour over ice in a punch bowl. Garnish with lemon wheels and jalapeño slices.

COGNAC

Today, many drinkers think of Cognac as a spirit best served unadulterated, the same way we regard Scotch. And there's nothing wrong with appreciating any Cognac on its own merits. (Or Scotch, for that matter.) But in the 19th century, Cognac was one of the most popular spirits for cocktails. Classics like the Sidecar and, by some accounts, the French 75 are Cognac-based; even cocktails we associate with whiskey, like the mint julep, were often made with Cognac.

These days, the main barrier to using Cognac in cocktails, at professional bars and home bars alike, tends to be the price—but several brands (among them Hine and Pierre Ferrand), appreciating the modern cocktail revolution, have released lower-priced blends made expressly for mixing, so there's no reason not to pick up a bottle.

SIDECAR

A classic that deserves to rank right up there with the daiquiri or the Negroni, this is one of those cocktails that's perfect in its simplicity. Just know that the Sidecar is bright and refreshing and easy to sip right down—yet carries a full three ounces of 80-proof liquor, so proceed with caution.

2 oz/60 mL H by Hine Cognac
1 oz/30 mL Pierre Ferrand dry Curaçao
1 oz/30 mL lemon juice

Combine all ingredients in cocktail shaker with ice. Shake until well chilled and strain into a coupe (with a sugared rim, if you wish). Garnish with a lemon twist.

THUG PASSION

Tom Dixon, Roberta's

Tupac, a vocal Cognac fan (of Hennessy in particular), christened a drink "Thug Passion" on his 1996 album *All Eyes On Me:* Cristal and Alizé Gold Passion, a Cognac-based passion-fruit liqueur. Tom Dixon's version brings in real fruit and Cognac, with high-quality orange liqueur, plus Prosecco—because we can't all drink Cristal every day.

1½ oz/45 mL Cognac
1½ oz/45 mL pineapple juice
½ oz/15 mL Combier orange liqueur
3 dashes Angostura bitters
Prosecco

Combine first three ingredients in a cocktail shaker with ice. Shake until well chilled and strain into a coupe. Top with prosecco. Dash the bitters on the foam and drag across foam with a straw.

COGNAC, RUM, AND RYE

Classic cocktails, by and large, tend to have a single base spirit, accented with modifiers (say, vermouth), citrus, and such. Split bases—when two or more full-fledged spirits play a role—are somewhat rarer. But Cognac is quite common in split-base cocktails, whether classics like a Vieux Carré or more modern inventions. Its soft, mellow character blends well with others, whether taming the spice in rye, or smoothly integrating with rum. (And given that it's such an expensive spirit, splitting the base is economical, too.)

VIEUX CARRÉ

Like many enduring classics, the Vieux Carré is the product of New Orleans, where it's still possible to find an excellent version of an often-overlooked drink.

¾ oz/20 mL Cognac
¾ oz/20 mL rye
¾ oz/20 mL Carpano Antica Formula
   sweet vermouth
¼ oz /10 mL Bénédictine
2 dashes Peychaud's bitters
2 dashes Angostura bitters

Combine all ingredients in a mixing glass with several cracked ice cubes. Stir until well chilled and strain into a rocks glass with one large ice cube. Garnish with a lemon twist.

TWELVE MILE LIMIT

Brian Smith, Colonie

"The Twelve Mile Limit is a cocktail we love for both its Prohibition-era history and its precise balance and blend of spirits," says Brian Smith. During Prohibition, alcohol was banned in the United States and in its territorial waters, up to twelve miles out—thus the name. Like the Sidecar, it drinks like an easygoing sour despite being a fully loaded cocktail.

1 oz/30 mL El Dorado 3 year rum
½ oz/15 mL Rittenhouse rye
½ oz/15 mL Paul Beau VS Cognac
½ oz/15 mL lemon juice
½ oz/15 mL grenadine (recipe p. 19)

Combine all ingredients in a cocktail shaker with ice. Shake until well chilled and strain into a martini glass or coupe. Garnish with a lemon twist.

Hotel Delmano

FORT DEFIANCE

A postindustrial, waterfront neighborhood that's a bit isolated, cleaved from the rest of Brooklyn by a highway, feeling even farther removed due to its distance from any subway, Red Hook is a distinct character in the New York landscape—which is exactly what endeared it to St. John Frizell. "I never wanted to live in New York until I saw this neighborhood," said Frizell, who moved to the city in 1999 and opened his Red Hook bar, Fort Defiance, in 2009. "It's got a small-town feel, but more than that, a maritime small-town feel—almost like a little fishing village."

As a Red Hook resident himself, Frizell knew what the neighborhood needed: somewhere to get "a good cup of coffee, a nice drink, and a place to take your mom when she's in town." And if you're going to serve food and drink, he believes, "why not make them really, really good?"

With no slight whatsoever to the kitchen (or the coffee), it's the cocktails that have earned the most acclaim. A historian through and through, Frizell sees cocktail history through the lens of the past, whether it's his obsession for the culinary and cocktail writer, world traveler, and general early-20th-century adventurer Charles H. Baker Jr., or his keen interest in classic cocktails and how to translate them for a modern drinking audience.

Classics were also a way for Fort Defiance to endear itself to the neighborhood. "I was concerned when I first opened that a fancy cocktail bar wouldn't work in Red Hook," he says. "So I put a Tom Collins on the menu, a Manhattan—some handles in the menu, drinks that people

who'd never been to a cocktail bar before can grab onto."

On the menu these days, you'll find a balance between straight-up classics, classically styled cocktails, and original creations. There's also a real focus on hot drinks, including a much-lauded Irish Coffee that will never go off the menu.

Ultimately, while Fort Defiance is in every way a modern cocktail bar, "I like thinking about cocktail history more than I like thinking about cocktail future," says Frizell. "There are some people who are very forward-thinking. I'm the reverse. I love to research, and find old drinks and rejigger their recipes and make them work for us . . . that's really the work that I enjoy. That's what gets me excited."

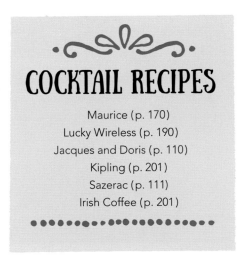

COCKTAIL RECIPES

Maurice (p. 170)
Lucky Wireless (p. 190)
Jacques and Doris (p. 110)
Kipling (p. 201)
Sazerac (p. 111)
Irish Coffee (p. 201)

> ❝I love to research, and find old drinks and rejigger their recipes and make them work for us ... That's what gets me excited.❞
>
> —*St. John Frizell, Fort Defiance*

FORT DEFIANCE was built in Red Hook during the Revolutionary War. Its four 18-pound cannon commanded New York Harbor & discouraged the British fleet from sailing into the East River during the Battle of Brooklyn. In August 1776, George Washington & the Continental Army narrowly escaped defeat at the hands of the British by crossing to Manhattan in the middle of the night, just a few miles upriver from Ft. Defiance.

WINDRUSH

Natasha David, Dear Bushwick

This stirred drink builds from its base of three spirits with an intriguing weighty, spiced chili-stout reduction.

1 oz/30 mL Rittenhouse Rye
¾ oz/20 mL Appleton VX rum
½ oz/15 mL Pierre Ferrand 1840 Cognac
¼ oz/10 mL chili-stout reduction
  (recipe p. 283)
4 drops Bittermens Mole bitters

Combine all ingredients in a mixing glass with ice. Stir until well chilled and strain into a rocks glass with fresh ice. Garnish with an orange twist.

LUCKY WIRELESS

Tyler Caffal, Fort Defiance

A (very) distant cousin of the little-known classic Marconi Wireless, this cocktail splits its base between Jamaican rum Appleton Reserve and Pierre Ferrand Cognac.

¾ oz/20 mL Appleton Reserve rum
¾ oz/20 mL Pierre Ferrand Cognac
¾ oz/20 mL Carpano Antica Formula
  sweet vermouth
¾ oz/20 mL Cinzano sweet vermouth
1 dash Peychaud's bitters
1 dash allspice dram

Combine all the ingredients in a mixing glass with ice. Stir until well chilled and strain into a coupe. Garnish with a lemon twist.

PISCO AND FRIENDS

CLASSIC PISCO SOUR

Rarely is a spirit so associated with a single drink as pisco with its sour. And it's a pretty appealing showcase for this unaged brandy: light, tart, and silky, with pisco's grape-y quality shining through. As limes in the States are different from the limes used in South America, many American bartenders prefer a mix of lemon and lime juice to try to approximate that flavor.

2 oz/60 mL pisco
½ oz/15 mL lemon juice
½ oz/15 mL lime juice
¾ oz/20 mL simple syrup
1 fresh egg white

Combine all ingredients in a cocktail shaker without ice. Shake vigorously for a "dry shake," then add ice and shake again. Strain into a coupe. Garnish with a lime wheel.

&TONIC

G in and tonic is a no-brainer. But the French often drink their Cognac with tonic water, for a drink as refreshing as it is elegant. Recipe at right—plus two other unexpected tonic pairings.

TONIC WATER

We don't have to use Schweppes or Canada Dry anymore—today, there are a number of high-quality tonics on the market, in specialty shops and many grocery stores. Fever Tree, Fentiman's, and Q Tonic are all good bets. Increasingly, you'll find tonic syrups, too—concentrated tonic flavor without the sparkling water. And some bartenders even make their own. (What sounds more "Brooklyn" than artisanal quinine syrup?)

COGNAC & TONIC

2 oz/60 mL Cognac
4 oz/120 mL tonic water

In a tall glass with ice, stir together the Cognac and tonic. Garnish with a lime wheel.

TEQUILA & TONIC

2 oz/60 mL blanco tequila
4 oz/120 mL tonic water

In a tall glass with ice, stir together the tequila and tonic. Squeeze in a lime wedge.

CHARTREUSE & TONIC

1½ oz/45 mL
yellow Chartreuse
4 oz/120 mL tonic water

In a tall glass with ice, stir together the Chartreuse and tonic. Garnish with a sprig of rosemary.

Sigani Spritz, Grand Ferry Tavern

LOVE MAKES YOU FEEL TEN FEET TALL

Jay Zimmerman, Ba'sik

As a clear spirit, pisco can make friends with other clear spirits, as in this pisco-gin combination made bittersweet through Aperol and Punt e Mes; neither the pisco nor the herbal gin is too dominant. As for the salt: Some bartenders integrate small amounts of salt into their cocktails to enliven and bring out flavors, just as a chef would.

1 oz/30 mL gin
¾ oz/20 mL pisco
¾ oz/20 mL Aperol
½ oz/15 mL Punt e Mes
2 to 3 drops salt water

Combine all the ingredients in a mixing glass with ice. Stir until well chilled and strain into a coupe. Garnish with an orange twist.

TO MAKE THE SALT WATER:

Add 2 tablespoons of table salt to a cup, and slowly add water while stirring, just until the salt dissolves partially. Strain the grainy mixture so the undissolved salt is separated from the very salty water. Put salinated water in dropper for use.

SINGANI SPRITZ

Grand Ferry Tavern

A close cousin of pisco, this Bolivian brandy, made from aromatic white Muscat of Alexandria grapes grown at high altitudes, is floral and a bit fruity—flavors that play well in the context of a spritz.

1 oz/30 mL Singani 63
½ oz/15 mL Aperol
½ oz/15 mL grapefruit juice
4 oz/120 mL sparkling rosé
   (Juve y Camp rose recommended)

Combine all ingredients except sparkling wine in a cocktail shaker with ice. Shake until well chilled and strain into a wine glass with fresh ice. Top with sparkling wine. Garnish with an orange twist.

BUENA ONDA

Ivy Mix, Leyenda

Ivy Mix infuses pisco with *yerba mate*, not only popular in South America, but also similar in taste profile to Peru's beloved coca leaf, which is, like mate, often consumed as a tea. Peruvian bartenders make coca pisco sours, but the ingredient is illegal in the States, so mate serves as the best substitute.

2 oz/60 mL yerba mate-infused Kappa
   pisco (recipe p. 269)
½ oz/15 mL lime juice
½ oz/15 mL lemon juice
¾ oz/20 mL simple syrup
½ oz/15 mL egg white
3 dashes hopped grapefruit bitters

Combine all ingredients in a cocktail shaker without ice. Shake vigorously for a "dry shake," then add ice and shake again. Strain into a coupe. Garnish with Angostura bitters, using a toothpick to draw hearts from the drops.

Tonia Guffey, Dram

APPLEJACK

"I'm a huge pusher of applejack," says Tonia Guffey of Dram. Unlike most other spirits, American apple brandy is dominated by one distillery—Laird's—beloved by many a bartender. "It's oldest commercial distillery in America," says Guffey; its license to distill, issued in 1780, is actually "License #1," the first granted in the new nation. George Washington and Abraham Lincoln were particular fans—and today, so are many modern bar-goers.

Laird's standard-issue applejack, tasty and affordable, is a mix of apple brandy and neutral grain spirit—but the good stuff is Laird's 100-proof Straight Apple Brandy, Bottled in Bond—made from apples and nothing else.

JACK ROSE

Tonia Guffey, Dram

"I'd like to see the Jack Rose get a little more love," says Guffey. It's a mighty appealing classic, with a gorgeous hue, strong on the applejack, brightened by citrus and sweetened with just enough high-quality grenadine. "Cherry garnish optional!"

2 oz/60 mL Laird's Bottled in Bond applejack
½ oz/15 mL lemon juice
½ oz/15 mL lime juice
½ oz/15 mL grenadine (recipe p. 19)
¼ oz/10 mL simple syrup

Combine all ingredients in a cocktail shaker with ice. Shake until well chilled and strain into a coupe.

TASKMASTER

Al Sotack, Jupiter Disco

Al Sotack's applejack cocktail is a complex union of bitter Maurin Quina and a profoundly smoky syrup made from lapsang souchong tea against the robust apple spirit, balanced and brightened by citrus juice and orange liqueur.

1½ oz/45 mL Laird's Bottled in
  Bond applejack
¼ oz/10 mL Maurin Quina
½ oz/15 mL lemon juice
½ oz/15 mL grapefruit juice
½ oz/15 mL lapsang syrup (recipe p. 278)
1 tsp/5 mL Grand Marnier

Combine all ingredients in a cocktail shaker with ice. Shake until well chilled and strain into a coupe. Garnish with a grapefruit wedge, and dash Angostura bitters on top.

APPLEJACK OLD FASHIONED

As a barrel-aged dark spirit, applejack shines in many of the same formats as whiskey—particularly something as simple as an Old Fashioned. Maple syrup is an ideal sweetener to pair with apples.

2 oz/60 mL Laird's Bottled in Bond applejack
¼ oz/10 mL maple syrup
2 dashes Angostura bitters
2 dashes orange bitters

Combine all ingredients in a mixing glass with several cracked ice cubes. Stir until well chilled and strain into a rocks glass with one large ice cube. Garnish with two lemon twists.

ENOCH'S FOLLY

Adam Volk, Esme

This Colorado-made brandy is distilled from green Bartlett pears, whose flavor is heightened with fresh pear juice and lemon and plays nicely with the botanicals of gin in this cocktail.

1 oz/30 mL CapRock Pear Brandy
¾ oz/20 mL gin
1 oz/30 mL Bartlett pear juice or
  pear nectar
¾ oz/20 mL lemon juice
½ oz/15 mL vanilla-demerara syrup
  (recipe p. 272)
¼ oz/10 mL almond syrup (can be
  store-bought)

Combine all the ingredients in a cocktail shaker with ice. Shake until well chilled and double-strain into a chilled coupe.

Patrons and bartender at The Drink

LOOSIE ROUGE

The sort of sleek, sexy cocktail bar that could thrive in Manhattan as easily as Brooklyn, Loosie Rouge opened in 2015 and immediately attracted the attention of a nightlife-savvy crowd; as the French might say, it's *très Brooklyn*.

"**The cocktails, and the bar, are all inspired by New Orleans ... But we bring our own touch to everything we do—whether it's an amaro, a new spice, the garnish, [or] the presentation.** "

– Arnaud Dissais, Loosie Rouge

Loosie's opening list was created by well-known French bartender Nico de Soto, of Manhattan's Experimental Cocktail Club and Mace; he tapped fellow countryman Arnaud Dissais, then the head bartender of fine-dining destination Daniel, to run and expand the program.

There's a sense of European cool that suffuses the space, despite its nominal New Orleans inspiration and distinct mid-century aesthetic, with artful layers of "torn" wallpaper, a low wood-paneled ceiling, and whitewashed brick walls.

"The cocktails, and the bar, are all inspired by New Orleans," says Dissais. "But we bring our own touch to everything we do—whether it's an amaro, a new spice, the garnish, the presentation." Many cocktails are on tap, an increasingly common practice, and many do have a distinctly modern, international bent: a julep with shiso leaves rather than mint; ingredients as diverse as sherry, cassis, and gin in a hibiscus iced tea. Even frozen drinks from a slushy machine, such as a plantain-rum concoction, are as sophisticated as they are fun—the goal of many a Brooklyn bar.

COCKTAIL RECIPES

Arnaud Palmer (p. 49)

Smoke and Mirror (p. 116)

Winter DRINKS

Here's the thing about a hot toddy: When you want one, you *really* want one.

Nothing combats bone-chilling cold in quite the same way, and nothing is as satisfying as letting the scented steam of an aromatic, boozy drink warm your face.

It's a different story on the other side of the bar—bringing in hot water, tea, or coffee can disrupt a busy bar's workflow—but those who embrace them, embrace them wholeheartedly. "When you walk into a bar and it's cold outside, the first thing you want is a hot drink," says St. John Frizell of Fort Defiance." Then we can move on to cocktails. But right now, give me something short and hot and *then* we can relax."

BRANDY TODDY

Bourbon does just as well here, but there's something even more comforting about a brandy toddy. In a hot drink, the steam lifts aromas from the cocktail and the garnish alike, so experiment with whatever spices in the cinnamon-allspice-clove genre you wish. (Star anise is unexpected and visually striking.)

2 oz/60 mL brandy
¼ oz/10 mL honey
1 dash Angostura bitters

In a heat-safe glass or mug, add the brandy, honey, and bitters. Pour 3 to 4 oz/90 to 120 mL of hot water over the top and stir until the honey is fully dissolved. Squeeze in a big lemon wedge. Garnish with warm spices, such as a cinnamon stick, cloves, and/ or allspice berries.

KIPLING
ZACH WHITE,
FORT DEFIANCE

Using the same "double boiler" technique as the Irish coffee at right, this hot buttered rum is improved with Curaçao, almondy orgeat, and fragrant allspice dram.

1½ oz/45 mL Appleton
Estate Reserve rum
½ oz/15 mL Pierre
Ferrand Curaçao
½ oz/15 mL orgeat
2 dashes allspice dram
1 tsp/5g salted butter

Combine all the ingredients in a mixing tin. Add boiling water to a mug to heat it, then nestle the tin in the mug so that the tin heats as well. Stir until the butter is dissolved, then discard water, pour contents of tin into the heated mug, and top with boiling water to just below the rim. Garnish with freshly grated nutmeg.

Irish Coffee, Fort Defiance

GOODNIGHT MOON
AISA SHELLY, RUCOLA

It's hard to imagine a more soothing drink than Cognac, warm milk and, again, winter-friendly allspice dram.

1½ oz/45 mL Cognac
¾ oz/20 mL honey syrup (1:1)
½ oz/15 mL allspice dram
3 oz/90 mL steamed milk

Combine all the ingredients a heat-safe mug. Dash on Angostura bitters and swirl to garnish.

IRISH COFFEE
ST. JOHN FRIZELL,
FORT DEFIANCE

None other than the *New York Times* once called St. John Frizell's Irish Coffee "the best in the known world"—which he wisely notes on Fort Defiance's cocktail menu.

1½ oz/45 mL Powers
Irish whiskey
1 oz/30 mL simple syrup
1 shot espresso
1½ oz/45 mL cream

Combine whiskey and simple syrup in a mixing tin. Add boiling water to a mug to heat it, and then nestle the tin in the mug so that the tin heats as well. Add the cream to a separate mixing tin and shake without ice until the cream thickens. Dump the water from the mug, add the whiskey-sugar mixture, and fill with boiling water to about 1 inch below the rim. Add the espresso (in a bar setting, pull the espresso shot right on top), and pour the thickened cream on top. Garnish with freshly grated cinnamon.

BRANDY, IN ALL ITS FORMS **201**

GRAND FERRY TAVERN

Joel Lee Kulp wasn't looking to open another bar so soon after the successful launch of The Richardson. But when an associate tipped him off to a Williamsburg space close to the waterfront, he immediately saw the potential.

"The inspiration was a classic American tavern," Kulp says, "in layout, in design, in concept. We talked about New York spots like White House Tavern and Corner Bistro . . . clams and burgers and steaks. And of course with elevated cocktails." There is indeed a bit of a time warp at Grand Ferry: aesthetically, musically, through its respect for lesser-known classic cocktails like the Martinez and the New York Sour. But unlike many bars of the moment, it's not overwhelmed by a mock-throwback feeling; it's just a comfortable tavern with old-world style.

As at The Richardson, cocktails are a priority; and each bar is essentially a team effort, according to Kulp. "When you step behind the bar, you'll see a glass filled with pieces of paper, everyone jotting down their ideas," he says; "I do direct, but this isn't about me putting my cocktail stamp on everything. The list depends so much on the staff."

And often, house cocktails are inspired by new spirits or liqueurs in the cocktail world—the Tokyo Fir, with Ransom Old Tom gin and the pine liqueur Zirbenz; the Singani Spritz, with a Bolivian grape brandy; or the Mount Sibillini Negroni, featuring a distinctive, limited-release herbal amaro.

While The Richardson has been longer established in Williamsburg, Kulp feels like Grand Ferry has made its own home in the neighborhood's western reaches. "Now that we've been here for two years, we have our own regulars, which is so wonderful," he says. "But this neighborhood changes so rapidly, and I'm starting to see old faces—people who will come in and feel comfortable, and sense a familiarity, and figure out, *You're the guy from The Richardson!*" Not a bad reputation to have.

COCKTAIL RECIPES

Tokyo Fir (p. 53)
Mt. Sibillini Negroni (p. 219)
The Big Red One (p. 93)
McGee's Nut Warmer (p. 117)
Free Fall (p. 141)
Singani Spritz (p. 192)

AMARO AND friends

How did such a specific class of liqueurs come to play such a huge role in mixology? Amari, broadly speaking—that's the plural of "amaro"—are Italian herbal liqueurs, traditionally consumed as an *aperitivo* (aperitif), to stimulate the appetite before dinner, or *digestivo* (digestif), to settle the stomach afterward. They run the spectrum from bright and orangey (amaro neophytes, try the sparkling Aperol Spritz, p. 212) to the dark, potent, and powerfully bitter (artichoke-based Cynar or the bartenders' eternal favorite, medicinal-herbal, palate-exploding Fernet-Branca).

On their own, amari deliver layers of bittersweet, herbal flavor, which makes them so ideal for sipping neat or with soda. But bartenders really love them in the context of cocktails, where even half an ounce can transform a drink with its nuance and complexity.

Campari is perhaps the best known amaro, and itself best known for the Negroni, an enduring classic. But today's bartenders have dozens more in their arsenals. Cozy up to a Brooklyn bar, ask about the barkeep's favorite amaro, and you're likely to get an earful—and perhaps a sip from a few bottles you've never heard of. (And then down a shot of Fernet.)

CHAPTER 8

MAISON PREMIERE

One part New Orleans, one part Brooklyn; one part 19th century, one part 21st; Maison Premiere is hard to characterize. But above all, according to bar manager Will Elliott, it should be "transportive."

"You're walking down the street in Williamsburg, maybe it's nice out, and we have our windows open, and you look straight through"—past the horseshoe bar, its green marble absinthe fountain, into a lush and, indeed, almost Southern-feeling garden. "It really does make you feel as if you've discovered a back garden in New Orleans."

> **"When we opened, we knew that we wanted to set our standards and expectations very high—and not necessarily limit ourselves to being a cocktail bar."**
>
> – *Will Elliott, Maison Premiere*

New Orleans through a century-old, heavily French-inflected lens, that is. "We had this notion of wanting to introduce old Parisian hospitality to a Brooklyn neighborhood that"—he pauses to phrase this correctly—"was still a bit, well, informal. Where casual bars were the norm."

No one could accuse Maison Premiere of being casual—from the period bartender garb to the elaborately garnished drinks and ornate absinthe fountains. (There may be no more Instagrammable bar in Brooklyn. Or

New York, for that matter.) They've earned two James Beard nominations, often considered the highest accolade in the culinary world.

The cocktail list is historically inspired—juleps, cobblers, and other classics make frequent appearances. But Elliott and bar director Maxwell Britten have no intention of being a museum. "Some cocktail bars are tomes of histories, in a bad way—where there's no notion of moving forward or participating," says Elliott. Not Maison Premiere; if there's a new high-end fruit liqueur or gentian aperitif on the American market, odds are it'll find its way to the menu.

Maison Premiere's aesthetic is immersive enough not to read as a theme; there's an internal consistency that really is, well, transportive. And its ambitions are staggering, even beyond its cocktails. "When we opened, we knew that we wanted to set our standards and expectations very high—and not necessarily limit ourselves to being a cocktail bar," according to Elliott. And they aren't—their list of Champagnes is 200 strong, their absinthe list the most extensive in the city (before we've even considered its excellent restaurant). Despite these extensive offerings, some choose to just rely on bartender expertise: "We have regulars who don't pay attention to the menu, but want to go through the cocktail history books. We can do that, too." And their oyster service—a dollar-oyster happy hour that draws lines around the block, with up to thirty-five oysters on the nightly menu—has its own following.

COCKTAIL RECIPES

Truth be told, Maison Premiere doesn't need dollar oysters to get people in the door. But it's one aspect of a bar they intend to be welcoming. "We wanted to be friendly, right from the get-go. We knew people might perceive as us as off-putting, somehow stiff or stodgy, or 'not a Brooklyn thing.'"

" It really does make you feel as if you've discovered a back garden in New Orleans. "

—*Will Elliott, Maison Premiere*

So, they feel, they've taken measures to combat that. "We're taking all our efforts to prepare. It's not your job to come in here and know a thing about our crazy oyster list, or all the absinthe that we have, or the two hundred-plus-bottle wine list; you can come in and have a beer for $7 if you want. There's no dress code; there's no door guy.

"We want to do everything we can, in terms of things we're passionate about—and hopefully do it without pretense."

APEROL SPRITZ

Few amari—truly, few spirits or liqueurs of any kind—are as likable as bright, barely bitter, rhubarb-orange Aperol. And the Aperol Spritz is an ideal cocktail for someone new to the world of these Italian liqueurs, showcasing Aperol's distinctive flavor in the context of a light, easy-drinking spritz. (The sparkling water might sound unnecessary, but is key for balance.)

3 oz/90 mL Prosecco
2 oz/60 mL Aperol
1 oz/30 mL sparkling water

Combine all the ingredients in large wine glass with ice and stir gently. Garnish with an orange slice.

CAPPELLETTI SPRITZ

Thanks to their bright red color and similar-sounding names, the Italian aperitif Cappelletti is often compared to Campari, but there's a true difference: It's wine-based rather than alcohol-based, lighter and a bit sweeter than Campari, vibrant but less aggressively bitter. It's well-suited to many cocktails, but is particularly easy to love in a spritz.

3 oz/90 mL Prosecco
2 oz/60 mL Cappelletti
1 oz/30 mL sparkling water

Combine all the ingredients in a large wine glass with ice and stir gently. Garnish with an expressed lemon wedge.

ASK ABOUT STUFF!

Sure, some bars are created by design consultants who pull in all sorts of trinkets and visual elements to suggest a casual, "authentic" look. But many Brooklyn bars are very personal spaces, designed by owners who put years into their vision and have a story for everything from the bar rail to the bathroom art. Without chatting up the bartenders, how would you know that those antique-looking whiskey bottles at The Drink were found in Babe Ruth's father's tavern—by one owner's father, who was excavating for Baltimore's Camden Yards when the tavern was unearthed? Or that Damon Boelte's collection of turkey figurines at Grand Army perch on a rafter, because the correct term for a group of turkeys is "a rafter of turkeys"? Or that the markings on Tooker Alley's bathroom door are from early-20th-century hobo symbology? If something catches your eye, odds are there's a story behind it.

Dear Bushwick

WHAT'S SO GREAT ABOUT FERNET-BRANCA?

It's become a cliché in recent years, but only because it's so true—bartenders go *nuts* for Fernet. (The term "Fernet" really refers to an entire genre of amari, but when you hear that word, it's usually referencing one brand: the Italian Fernet-Branca.) How exactly to describe Fernet? It's mouthwash and cough syrup, bitter and herbal and licorice-y, mint-y and pine-y… it's a mouthful of contradictions in each tidy, yet overpowering, shot.

Watch at your favorite cocktail bar and, if you stick around long enough, odds are good you'll see a bartender knocking back a shot of Fernet. (And odds are, whoever they're knocking back that shot with is also in the industry.)

So what explains the obsession? There's a certain "I'm in the club," "yeah, I can take it" quality, to be sure. There's no disputing that Fernet is an acquired taste, so ordering a Fernet shot suggests that, well, you've already acquired said taste. It's also well suited to drinking behind the bar; Fernet is the same proof as vodka or tequila, but goes down differently than a spirit. While there's little or no evidence that different alcohols actually result in different "kinds" of inebriation, Fernet, just by virtue of its flavor, is a slap in the face and a rush of energy—invigorating, not sedating.

What's more, bartenders tend to be flavor junkies. After all, much of their job is appreciating flavor and understanding how to deploy it; bartenders tend to have a greater appreciation than most for hyper-smoky Scotches and mezcals, for unusual new liqueurs, for pungent shrubs. And it's hard to imagine a bigger hit of flavor—for better or worse—than Fernet.

3 { FERNET SHOT ALTERNATIVES

Maybe you just can't take the intensity of Fernet; maybe you've had so many Fernet shots in your day, you've tired of them. Here are a few alternatives that deliver a similar bitter-herbal pick-me-up.

CIA
DRAM

""One of the drinks we created that's become a bit of an underground bartender shot is the CIA," says Tonia Guffey. "I wanted the proof like Fernet, but I wanted a break from it. So I decided to take Cynar, which is slightly low in proof, and bonded applejack, which is higher, and I put them together 50/50 split, added a drop of Angostura, and boom, a shot was born."

1 oz/30 mL Cynar
1 oz/30 mL Laird's Bottled in Bond applejack
1 dash Angostura bitters

Combine the ingredients and pour into a large shot glass (for a big shot) or two shot glasses (for a moderate one).

ANGOSTURA AND RUM

Bartenders have been known to take shots of Angostura bitters on their own—intensely spiced and just as bitter as you'd expect. Tasty in its rather extreme way, though it dries out your mouth. This shot juxtaposes a heavy pour of Ango with full-bodied, rich añejo rum, its sweetness an ideal balance.

1½ oz/45 mL Ron Zacapa 23 rum (or a similar weighty añejo)
½ oz/15 mL Angostura bitters

Combine the ingredients and pour into a large shot glass (for a big shot) or two shot glasses (for a moderate one).

RYE & MONTENEGRO

Using a 100-proof rye gives this shot serious power, while the amaro Montenegro contributes a bit of body and its distinctive orange character.

1½ oz/45 mL Rittenhouse rye
½ oz/15 mL Montenegro amaro

Combine the ingredients and pour into a large shot glass (for a big shot) or two shot glasses (for a moderate one).

MONTENEGRO SPRITZ

More robust and boozier than Aperol, Montenegro is a bit less sweet and even bigger on the orange, and makes just as compelling a spritz.

3 oz/90 mL Prosecco
2 oz/60 mL Montenegro
1 oz/30 mL sparkling water

Combine all the ingredients in large wine glass with ice and stir gently. Garnish with an orange slice.

BRANCOLADA
Jeremy Oertel, Donna

"Our most popular cocktail of all time," says beverage manager Jeremy Oertel. "By orders of magnitude." When Oertel worked at Dram, the bar had a Branca Menta chilling machine, and waitresses used to pour it on top of ice cream sandwiches. It was so delicious, he attests, that it inspired this creamy-minty cocktail with a tropical bent. (Truth be told, it resembles a Painkiller more closely than a Piña Colada, but according to Oertel, only the strictest cocktail geeks will point that out; and Colada is just a better name to riff on.)

1 oz/30 mL Branca Menta
1 oz/30 mL Appleton V/X Jamaican Rum
1½ oz/45 mL pineapple juice
¼ oz/10 mL orange juice
¾ oz/20 mL coconut cream (3 parts
   Coco Lopez to 1 part coconut milk)

Combine all the ingredients in a cocktail shaker with ice. Shake until well chilled and strain into a hurricane glass with crushed ice. Garnish with a mint sprig and an orange wedge.

ROAD TO NOWHERE
Adam Volk, Esme

Amari deliver complex flavor on their own, but also tend to pair up well with each other, as in this whiskey-amaro stirred drink that brings together Luxardo Abano (herbaceous with prominent orange and cardamom) and the Campari-like Luxardo bitter.

1 oz/30 mL Luxardo Abano
1 oz/30 mL Luxardo bitter (or Campari)
1 oz/30 mL Old Overholt rye
4 dashes Regan's orange bitters

Combine all the ingredients in a mixing glass with ice. Stir until well chilled and strain into a chilled coupe. Garnish with a brandied cherry.

ONE MORE THAT'S IT
Rob Krueger, Extra Fancy

Named for a customer who would declare "One more, that's *it*" when ordering one of these boozy stirred drinks—and promptly ask for another not too long after the cocktail—demonstrates the affinity of amaro for whiskey.

1 oz/30 mL Meletti amaro
1¼ oz/40 mL Four Roses bourbon
¾ oz/20 mL El Dorado 8 Year rum
2 dashes mole bitters

Combine all the ingredients in a mixing glass with ice. Stir until well chilled and strain into a rocks glass with fresh ice. Garnish with an orange twist.

Hotel Delmano

TAKES ON THE NEGRONI

Once you've developed a taste for the bittersweet, herbal nuances of amari, the Negroni will quickly become a favorite. Each of its components contributes an herbaceousness; vermouth and Campari, just enough sweetness to balance; a big orange twist, a burst of citrus oils to enliven the whole thing. It's also one of the easiest cocktails to riff on: Instead of gin, why not whiskey (for a Boulevardier)? Instead of Campari, why not Aperol, or Cynar, or a lesser-known amaro?

CLASSIC NEGRONI

Use a classic London dry gin like Beefeater and an excellent sweet vermouth like Carpano Antica Formula, and you're on your way. 1-1-1 is the classic ratio, well-balanced and easy to remember, though many bartenders will up the gin to 1½ oz/45 mL, to make this cocktail a bit more robust; try it both ways and see which you prefer.

1 oz/30 mL Beefeater gin
1 oz/30 mL Carpano Antica Formula sweet vermouth
1 oz/30 mL Campari

Combine all the ingredients in a mixing glass with several cracked ice cubes. Stir until well chilled and strain into a rocks glass with one large ice cube. Garnish with an expressed orange peel.

Crown Heights Negroni, Tooker Alley

Capone's Cocktail, Pork Slope

THE BOULEVARDIER

TOBY CECCHINI,
LONG ISLAND BAR

Toby Cecchini's carefully honed take on the Boulevardier uses two ryes and two sweet vermouths, with the full 2 oz/60 mL of rye assuming the leading role.

**1 oz/30 mL Rittenhouse Bonded 100-Proof rye
1 oz/30 mL Old Overholt rye
1 oz/30 mL Campari
⅔ oz/20 mL Cinzano Rosso sweet vermouth
⅓ oz/10 mL Carpano Antica Formula sweet vermouth**

Combine all the ingredients in a mixing glass with ice. Stir well, at least 1 minute, until well chilled. Strain into a chilled cocktail coupe. Garnish with a twist of lemon.

RUCOLA NEGRONI

CABELL TOMLINSON,
RUCOLA

A classic Negroni uses medium-bodied, moderately bitter Campari; Rucola's version goes in opposing, complementary directions with lighter, orangier Aperol and darker, more powerfully bitter Cynar.

**1 oz/30 mL London dry gin
1 oz/30 mL Aperol
1 oz/30 mL Cynar**

Combine all the ingredients in a mixing glass with ice. Stir until well chilled and strain into a coupe. Garnish with an orange twist.

CAPONE'S COCKTAIL

JOHN BUSH, PORK SLOPE

A simple, no-frills Boulevardier riff for those less inclined toward rye, with easy-drinking (and very affordable) Evan Williams bourbon.

**2 oz/60 mL Evan Williams bourbon
1 oz/30 mL Campari
1 oz/30 mL Carpano Antica Formula sweet vermouth
1 dash Angostura bitters**

Combine all the ingredients in a mixing glass with ice. Stir until well chilled and strain into a rocks glass with fresh ice, or if preferred, a coupe. Garnish with an orange twist.

MT. SIBILLINI NEGRONI
GRAND FERRY TAVERN

Just swapping out a single ingredient is a fun way to play with a Negroni; this version showcases the rooty, strongly herbal amaro Sibilla against the standard gin and sweet vermouth.

1 oz/30 mL City of London dry gin
1 oz/30 mL Sibilla amaro
1 oz/30 mL Dolin sweet vermouth

Combine all the ingredients in a mixing glass with ice. Stir until well chilled and strain into a chilled coupe. Garnish with a lemon twist.

CROWN HEIGHTS NEGRONI
DEL PEDRO, TOOKER ALLEY

Del Pedro's Negroni uses the Brooklyn-made liqueur Sorel for an even more vibrant red hue and a faint trace of hibiscus in the background.

1½ oz/45 mL Junipero gin
½ oz/15 mL Carpano Antica Formula sweet vermouth
½ oz/15 mL Campari
½ oz/15 mL Sorel liqueur

Combine all the ingredients in a mixing glass with several cracked ice cubes. Stir until well chilled and strain into a Nick and Nora glass. Garnish with a dehydrated orange slice.

VIDA DE MOLE
GRAN ELECTRICA

"This is our Mexican spin on a Negroni," says co-owner Tamer Hamawi, "substituting mezcal and bringing in slightly sweet chocolate bitters to round out that spirit's smokiness."

1 oz/30 mL Del Maguey Vida mezcal
1 oz/30 mL Campari
1 oz/30 mL sweet vermouth
2 dashes Bittermens Xocolatl Mole bitters

Combine all the ingredients in a mixing glass with ice. Stir until well chilled and strain into a rocks glass with fresh ice. Garnish with an orange twist.

WHISKEY SKIFFER
BRIAN FLOYD, THE VANDERBILT

For those who love Boulevardiers, try one with the rich, bitter, artichoke-based Cynar.

1 oz/30 mL Old Overholt rye
1 oz/30 mL Cynar
1 oz/30 mL Carpano Antica Formula sweet vermouth
2 to 3 drops chocolate bitters

Combine all the ingredients in a mixing glass with ice. Stir until well chilled and strain into a coupe. Garnish with an orange twist.

GRAND ARMY

If ever there were a neighborhood eager for an easygoing yet top-notch cocktail bar, it was Boerum Hill, a pleasant residential area tucked right next to downtown Brooklyn. And if ever there were a person to do it, that was Damon Boelte, with a serious track record in the Brooklyn bar world, and partners with their own local credentials: Julian Brizzi of popular Italian spot Rucola, Noah Bernamoff of beloved nouveau-deli Mile End, and photographer Daniel Krieger.

During his time at Prime Meats in Carroll Gardens, Boelte had developed a reputation as an innovative mixologist—but his interest in cocktails dates back much longer. "I've been collecting cocktail books since I was eleven years old," he says. "When I was still a kid, I shoplifted a bottle of Angostura bitters, just because I wanted to know what alcohol tasted like." (Perhaps needless to say, trying a shot of unadulterated Angostura put him off for a few years.)

A decade later, Boelte had "blasted through" virtually every one of his professional passions—worked in graphic design, owned a vintage motorcycle and scooter shop, run a specialty guitar shop—by the time he was 22 years old. In that time, he was a cocktail hobbyist, hosting parties with Manhattans and margaritas light-years beyond what his Oklahoma friends were familiar with. He eventually came to the other side of the bar, then moved to New York; working at industry-favorite liquor store LeNell's, he met the owners of Frankies 457, who then opened Prime Meats, where Boelte worked for years.

It's easy to see his fingerprints on Grand Army; there's a casual vibe to the light-filled corner space, but once you start looking, a serious design element too. And once you get him talking, the relatively new bar houses endless stories. "I'm really into things that are unique to the bar," he says—his cabinet of exceedingly rare spirits, his copper bar tools and Waterford coupes. Lest that sound overly stuffy, Boelte's tiki mug and accessory game is equally strong; his collection of turkey figurines perch along a rafter; he uses blue-and-white

> ❝ I want Grand Army to be light, bright, playful, welcoming— a very, very warm place. ❞
> —Damon Boelte, Grand Army

speckled camp cups for hot drinks. ("I'm still an Okie farm boy at heart.") Bartenders occasionally sport Hawaiian shirts; a slow Monday night might have Boelte blowing up beach balls, just for a good time—"I want Grand Army to be light, bright, playful, welcoming—a very, very warm place."

Cocktails reflect this skilled-but-inclusive philosophy, from the bourbon-Lillet-champagne American Royal Zepyhr to the gin-Aperol-citrus Trans-Siberian—thoughtful modern, likable. "There might not be everything for everyone. But I do want *something* for everyone."

COCKTAIL RECIPES

3

LOW-PROOF AMARO COCKTAILS

For all their intensity of flavor, amari tend to be lower in alcohol than spirits, which makes them ideal for low-proof cocktails, when you want to enjoy a few drinks without quite the level of inebriation.

AMERICANO
TONIA GUFFEY, DRAM

"I like my Americanos to be more heavy on the club soda," says Dram's Tonia Guffey, who suggests a 1:1:3 Campari–vermouth–club soda ratio; more common is 1:1:2, but feel free to use as much or as little soda as you wish.

1 oz/30 mL Campari
1 oz/30 mL Dolin sweet vermouth
Club soda

In a rocks glass or Collins glass with ice (depending on how much club soda you're pouring), briefly stir together the Campari and vermouth and top with soda. Garnish with a long orange twist.

MILANO TORINO
THE NARROWS

"People who haven't ever had an amaro like this drink because the vermouth really calms the Fernet down and susses out the flavors underneath the extra-bitter, mouthwash-y thing it's famous for."

2 oz/60 mL Carpano Antica Formula sweet vermouth
1 oz/30 mL Fernet-Branca
Club soda

In a tall glass with ice, stir together all the ingredients. Garnish with a lemon twist.

CYNAR & GRAPEFRUIT

A flavor powerhouse all on its own, Cynar pairs very well with grapefruit juice, each echoing the other's bitter-sweet character; Cynar, grapefruit, and soda makes for a super-complex, low-proof drink that you can sip one after another for hours.

1 oz/30 mL Cynar
1½ oz/45 mL grapefruit juice
Club soda

In a tall glass with ice, stir together all the ingredients. Garnish with a lemon twist.

LONDON'S BURNING

Darren Grenia, Dear Bushwick

Once you've developed a taste for the bitter, Amaro Braulio is not only compelling, but fascinating: Bitter orange, star anise, peppermint, and more all weave together in a liqueur that invites more and more tastes, just to try it again. Its multifaceted, sharp flavors peek through Darren Grenia's cocktail, with smoky Islay Mist blended Scotch and a bit of tawny port to sweeten.

1½ oz/45 mL Braulio amaro
1 oz/30 mL Islay Mist blended Scotch whisky
¼ oz/10 mL Dow's Fine tawny port
1 dash orange bitters

Combine all the ingredients in a mixing glass with ice. Stir until well chilled and strain into a double rocks glass with fresh ice. Garnish with a flamed orange peel (recipe p. 29).

ARCH LEVELER

Justin Olsen, Bearded Lady

"A vegetal and smoky cooler," the drink's creator Justin Olsen calls it; "perfect for bridge seasons when days are warm and nights are cold."

1 oz/30 mL Cynar
1 oz/30 mL vodka
½ oz/15 mL lemon juice
½ oz/15 mL ginger syrup (recipe p. 273)
½ oz/15 mL Laphroaig Islay 10 Year
  Scotch whisky
Club soda

Combine all the ingredients except club soda in a Collins glass over crushed or cracked ice. Stir well, add more ice to fill, and top with soda and 2 dashes of Angostura bitters. Garnish with a mint sprig and a lemon twist.

Maison Premiere

Dram

AND SODA

When you encounter a powerful herbal liqueur with bitter, concentrated flavors, it's pretty ambitious to start drinking it straight. Often, the solution is soda—which lightens and brightens the amaro, leaving you with a refreshing drink that's only gently bitter.

CAMPARI & SODA

1½ oz / 45 mL Campari
4 oz / 120 mL soda water

In a tall glass with ice, stir together the Campari and soda. Squeeze in an orange wedge.

CYNAR & SODA

1½ oz / 45 mL Cynar
4 oz / 120 mL soda water

In a tall glass with ice, stir together the Cynar and soda. Garnish with a grapefruit wedge.

FERNET & COKE

A favorite in Argentina, the world's biggest fan of Fernet-Branca (other than the bartending community), where it's called *fernet con coca*.

1½ oz / 45 mL
Fernet-Branca
4 oz / 120 mL Coca-Cola

In a tall glass with ice, stir together Fernet and Coke. Garnish with a lemon twist.

DRAM

In 2010, many of the city's best-regarded cocktail bars—which, at the time, meant Manhattan—were all about the speakeasy aesthetic: low-lit, jazz music, bartenders with suspenders and pencil mustaches. But Dram, which opened that year in South Williamsburg, was having none of it. "Our goal was to get out of that precious, fancier side of bartending," says beverage director and bar manager Tonia Guffey, "and do something more current—but still make really, really good drinks."

Years later, it's regarded as one of the first bars to do so successfully; and its dual laid-back attitude and mixology reputation made it an industry favorite—the bar that bartenders go to when they're off-duty. Throwback hip-hop on the sound system, young bartenders sans uniforms—Dram not only eschewed formality, but pushed the needle in the opposite direction. "We're a rowdy, raucous bunch," says Guffey. "We'll play *Road House* and listen to rap. I really think it's a more of a Williamsburg feel."

And as its notoriety as a bar grew, so did its cocktail reputation. Dram's opening staff came from many of Manhattan's heavyweight bars—PDT, Flatiron Lounge, Pegu Club—and brought different perspectives from across an industry still very much evolving. "We each had a school that we learned under, and our own bar mentors, and all of that came in to Dram," says Guffey. "We mashed it all up." And Dram itself is now a line item on the resumes of many well-known bar folks. "It's a huge part of what we do—find up-and-coming people, give them a home here, hopefully help them learn something, and throw them out in the world."

In terms of a cocktail list, Dram keeps it short—six to eight drinks—with the implication that their bartenders are capable of much more. "We can really focus on each drink, and work it through many, many times until we get something we're happy with," says Guffey. "But we can make everything." An early proponent of "bartender's choice," which was on Dram's menu when it opened, Guffey sees the bar emphasizing that "even if you don't know what you want to drink, we can get you where you want to be."

COCKTAIL RECIPES

New Ceremony (p. 105)

King Medicine (p. 158)

Jack Rose (p. 193)

❝ We can really focus on each drink, and work it through many, many times until we get something we're happy with ...**❞**

—*Tonia Guffey, Dram*

Higgins' Sarsparilla, The Richardson

HIGGINS' SARSPARILLA
The Richardson

Rich and on the sweeter side, as amari go, Averna is a liqueur that even relative amaro newcomers can drink straight, so a heavy pour works quite well in this ginger-amaro cocktail with a red wine float.

1¾ oz/50 mL Averna amaro
¼ oz/10 mL Beaujolais red wine
Fentiman's ginger beer

Add the Averna to a double rocks glass with ice. Top with ginger beer, then float the wine on top. Garnish with a lemon twist.

COOL LEATHERETTE
Jonny Sela, Sisters

"There's something a little rough and ready about this cocktail," says Sela, where the spice of rye and ginger meet the bittersweet, aromatic Ramazzotti. "We could have used some kind of shrub to introduce the vinegar, but somehow good old balsamic makes drinking this a bit more fun."

1½ oz/45 mL rye
1½ oz/45 mL Ramazzotti amaro
¾ oz/20 mL lime juice
¾ oz/20 mL ginger syrup (recipe p. 273)
¼ oz/10 mL balsamic vinegar

Combine the first four ingredients in a cocktail shaker with ice. Shake until well chilled and strain into a rocks glass with fresh ice. Drizzle with balsamic and garnish with two brandied cherries.

LA TEMPESTA
Demetrius Goosbey, Franny's

This upscale Park Slope pizzeria's cocktail menu often plays with amari; here, a little bit of Fernet-Branca plays to great effect, paired with the comparatively tamer, pleasantly herbal Nonino. Mint picks up those herbal flavors, while ginger beer contributes a warm spice.

1 oz/30 mL Nonino amaro
½ oz/15 mL Fernet-Branca
½ oz/15 mL mint syrup (recipe p. 277)
¾ oz/20 mL lemon juice
Ginger beer

Combine the first four ingredients in a cocktail shaker with ice. Shake until well chilled and strain into a Collins glass with fresh ice. Top with ginger beer. Garnish with a lemon twist.

3
PIMM'S COCKTAILS

WIRE + STRING
MAKS PAZUNIAK,
JUPITER DISCO

The UK's favorite summer drink, the Pimm's Cup is built from a base of its namesake, a gin-based liqueur that's a bit herbal, a bit spiced, quite citrusy—not *all* that far off from an amaro. Pimm's and Campari pair up for the base of a refreshing tall drink that's a bit more robust than the classic Pimm's.

1¼ oz/40 mL Pimm's No. 1
1¼ oz/40 mL Campari
¾ oz/20 mL lemon juice
½ oz/15 mL pineapple syrup
(recipe p. 273)
Club soda

Combine all the ingredients except club soda in a cocktail shaker with ice. Shake until well chilled and strain into a Collins glass with fresh ice. Top with soda.

STANDARD
PIMM'S CUP

There may be no better drink for a summer afternoon than the classic Pimm's Cup. The traditional version couldn't be easier: Pimm's with English-style carbonated lemonade or perhaps ginger ale.

2 oz/60 mL Pimm's No. 1
4 oz/120 mL ginger ale or
carbonated lemonade

Combine the ingredients in a glass with ice and stir. Garnish with a cucumber slice and a strawberry.

AMPED-UP
PIMM'S CUP

Nothing wrong with a basic Pimm's Cup—so simple you could make one even after already having imbibed a few. But it's a fun drink to take into cocktail territory; Pimm's is a gin-based liqueur, so why not add some gin? It invites fruit garnish, so why not up the fruit?

1 oz/30 mL Pimm's No. 1
1 oz/30 mL Beefeater gin
¼ oz/10 mL lemon juice
¼ oz/10 mL simple syrup
3 mint leaves
1 strawberry (plus
more for garnish)
1 slice cucumber (plus
more for garnish)
2 oz/60 mL ginger beer

In the bottom of a cocktail shaker, muddle the cucumber and strawberry. Add ice, the Pimm's, gin, lemon, simple syrup, and mint, and shake until well chilled. Double-strain into a Collins glass with fresh ice and top with the ginger beer. Garnish with another cucumber slice, half a strawberry, a mint sprig, and a lemon wheel.

BEER, WINE, AND BUBBLES

When you pop a can of beer or uncork a bottle of wine, odds are you're planning to enjoy that drink on its own. But beer and wine can integrate beautifully into cocktails, too. Sparkling wine, of course, is essential for numerous drinks, from the Aperol Spritz to the French 75. But recently, bartenders have experimented with still wines as well. Many cocktail ingredients are themselves wine-based, from vermouths to aperitifs like Lillet to grape brandies, and become natural pairings. Depending on the wine, it can add acidity, fruit flavors, herbal or earthy flavors—all characteristics a mixologist might want to play with in a cocktail. And beer, too, not only adds lift and carbonation, but can contribute the piney, herbal hops of an IPA or the weight and heft of a stout.

COCKTAILS
* MICHELADA   -10
* BRAMBUN' MAN   -11
                 -9/26
* EAST ENDER   -11
* CANTALOUPE SHANDY - 11
  'N DRANK   - 12

>>CANS
* BUDWEISER $ Five
* 12·03 MODELO $ 5
* BITBURGER $ 7.0
  EAST CIDER $ 7 00

HOUR
FROZEN
DRINK

MON-FRI 4-7PM
$ 20 00 PROSECCO
        BOTTLES
$ 20 00 PACIFICO
        BUCKETS

CHAPTER 9

235

ROBERTA'S

The first culinary destination, so to speak, in the largely industrial neighborhood of Bushwick, Roberta's is best known as a pizzeria, then a restaurant, then a wine destination . . . or perhaps a restaurant, then a pizzeria and bakery, then a wine destination? Launched at a time when most Manhattan-dwellers couldn't find Bushwick on a subway map, Roberta's got its start in 2008 as a pizzeria that quickly earned enough accolades to lure curious food obsessives out on the L train. But its kitchen's interests didn't stop at pizza, and it evolved into a fully fledged restaurant with what, at times, seemed like outsized ambitions. An onsite garden fed the kitchen's creativity; its wine list, heavy on natural and little-known bottles, earned acclaim of its own.

" When it's sunset and you feel the breeze, the foosball table and the frozen drink machine— it's such a special place to hang out. " —Tom Dixon, Roberta's

In all Roberta's endeavors, cocktails hadn't really figured in. But, says bar manager Tom Dixon, why shouldn't that change? "We're a 'rolling restaurant,' you could say; things just sort of happen. We're always tweaking and probing and searching." So while cocktails

hadn't fit into Roberta's initial purview, the restaurant had never really confined itself to others' expectations, either. "Our wine director is incredible—but if you're out on a Friday night, you're probably going to want to start with a cocktail."

When Dixon joined the team four years back, Roberta's didn't even hire daytime bartenders; "The servers would just go behind the bar at lunch and make drinks. There wasn't much of a list, we'd just screw around in the afternoon, when it was quiet." But that sort of experimentation eventually led to drinks that Dixon grew excited about.

While the bar itself wasn't large enough to support a huge liquor selection, Roberta's offered plenty of other avenues for cocktail development. "Melissa, our gardener, is an incredible resource, as is having such intelligent people in the kitchen." As a result, his cocktails lean heavily on house infusions and liqueurs; everything from strawberry shrubs and cantaloupe liqueur to cucumber–pink peppercorn vodka and coconut rum, even making their own vermouth—in the DIY, experimental, homegrown spirit of the restaurant as a whole.

This supports two essentially distinct bars— one inside, serving drinks in the restaurant proper; and an outdoor "tiki bar" that, in the words of Dixon, tends to be "party central" "Outside, it's a weird tucked-away spot and such a unique feel. When it's sunset and you

feel the breeze, the foosball table and the frozen drink machine—it's such a special place to hang out."

Inside, cocktails with a bit more of a culinary focus, like the Stone of Jordan; outside, plastic cups with chuggable drinks like the East Ender and Cantaloupe Shandy are served alongside buckets of beer. That two different styles exist in the same restaurant is just one more illustration of how multifaceted, and how singular, Roberta's has come to be.

COCKTAIL RECIPES

Stone of Jordan (p. 66)
Cantaloupe Shandy (p. 243)
East Ender (p. 71)
Belafonte (p. 138)
Thug Passion (p. 184)
Significant Other (p. 158)

Fort Defiance

BEER

CLASSIC MICHELADA

A drink with infinite variations throughout Mexico and beyond, the Michelada is a beer cocktail spiked with lime, often tomato juice or Clamato (a canned clam broth–tomato drink), and any number of other flavorings and spices. It's worth trying out the straight-forward tomato-cerveza before getting into the variations.

6 oz/180 mL tomato juice
6 oz/180 mL Mexican lager
1 oz/30 mL lime juice
6 to 8 dashes hot sauce (Tabasco for intense heat; Tapatio or Cholula will be milder)

Rim a pint glass with coarse salt, if desired. Combine all the ingredients in a glass with ice and stir briefly. Adjust the hot sauce to taste. Garnish with a lime wedge.

MI MICHELADA
Gran Electrica

"The recipes for Micheladas differ greatly around Central America, but we love the addition of Clamato for the tangy, zesty flavor it gives. Valentina is our hot sauce of choice; it has a great consistency for lining the inside of the glass." While Gran Electrica rims the glass with a celery salt–pequin pepper mixture, celery salt (or even regular salt) will work, too.

6 dashes Valentina hot sauce
4 dashes Worcestershire sauce
2 oz/60 mL Clamato
1 oz/30 mL lime juice
1 12-oz/360-mL can Tecate

Rim a pint glass with a mixture of celery salt and coarse salt, if desired. Dash the hot sauce around the inside of the glass, fill the glass with ice, then add the Clamato, lime, and Worcestershire. Pour Tecate over to fill. Garnish with a long cucumber stick, cut longer than the pint glass is tall. If some beer remains in the can, top up as you drink.

BEER AND A SHOT

" What do cocktail bartenders drink when they go to bars? Honestly, a shot and a beer... "
—David Moo, Quarter Bar

"What do cocktail bartenders drink when they go to bars? Honestly, a shot and a beer," according to David Moo of Quarter Bar. We asked bartenders about their favorite combos.

"11211," LITTLE KINGS CREAM ALE AND ROCK AND RYE
EXTRA FANCY

"Little Kings is a classic American cream ale that marries perfectly with the bright grain, sweet cherry, and vanilla of the Rock and Rye. 11211 is the zip code we share with New York Distilling Company and of course, Brooklyn is in New York's Kings County."

HARPOON AND FERNET
THE DRINK

"We love a beer and a shot. We resisted putting them on the menu for a few years, but gave in when we started carrying Harpoon Cider. We're huge cider fans here, and the Harpoon is a crisp, easy one, well made, with enough residual sugar to pull in the sweet cider folks, but not so sweet that it puts off the craft cider people. We sell it as a special with a shot of Fernet-Branca, a pretty perfect bitter-sweet pairing we stumbled on with the help of one of our old beer guys."

WIDOW JANE BOURBON AND SARATOGA LAGER
Tooker Alley

"A classic bourbon and beer love match between Red Hook's own Widow Jane bourbon, from Cacao Prieto, and blue-collar Saratoga Lager."

241

Cantaloupe Shandy, Roberta's

KIMCHILADA

Torrey Bell-Edwards, Willow

"The Kimchilada is a take on the Mexican classic," says beverage director Torrey Bell-Edwards, "using primarily Korean ingredients, and works as a savory, spicy pick-me-up." While some Micheladas are only half beer, the "kimchilada" mix is intense enough that a little goes a long way.

KIMCHILADA MIX

16 oz/480 mL lime juice
8 oz/240 mL kimchi juice (poured from jar of kimchi)
2½ oz/80 mL gochujang, Korean fermented chili paste (or other chili paste)
4 oz/120 mL soy sauce
4 oz/120 mL mirin cooking wine

COCKTAIL

Rim a pint glass with salt, gently fill halfway with Modelo Especial beer, and add 1 oz/30 mL kimchilada mix. Top with ice and garnish with a lime wedge.

CLASSIC SHANDY

A refreshing blend of beer and a nonalcoholic partner—whether lemonade, ginger ale, or similar—the shandy is an ideal beer cocktail for day drinking, whether at a summer picnic, after a long bike ride, or any comparable moment. Plenty of breweries sell bottled shandies, but making your own, which couldn't be easier, lets you determine how sweet, tart, or boozy you'd like yours.

6 oz/180 mL beer (pilsner recommended)
4 oz/120 mL fresh lemonade (or combine 1 oz/30 mL lemon juice, ½ oz/15 mL simple syrup, and 2½ oz/65 mL water)

Combine all the ingredients in a pint glass with ice and stir briefly. Garnish with a lemon wedge.

CANTALOUPE SHANDY

Tom Dixon, Roberta's

Crisp, lively wheat beers like Witte are often served with a lemon slice; this shandy echoes that pairing with lime and a strong dose of freshly made cantaloupe liqueur. Refreshing and dangerously drinkable.

3 oz/90 mL cantaloupe liqueur (recipe p. 270)
½ oz/15 mL lime juice
Ommegang Witte beer

Fill a pint glass with ice and add the cantaloupe liqueur and lime. Top with about 6 oz/180 mL beer.

DEAR BUSHWICK

Dear Bushwick was originally conceived as an "English country kitchen," and to some extent it does look the part of a snug pub. But Oxfordshire pubs don't have as extensive an amaro collection as Dear Bushwick, or cocktails with mezcal and chile-stout syrup, or such an ambitious cocktail-on-tap program in the works.

The kitchen has earned a good deal of acclaim—it's actually listed in the Michelin guide, which still seems a bit odd for Bushwick—but the cocktails have their own following. The list was first designed by acclaimed mixologist Natasha David, but is now run by bar director Darren Grenia, a partner of owner Julian Mohamed. "It started out gin and rum heavy," he says, "but since then I've opened it up—we have no restrictions."

As at many venues, the kitchen and bar play off each other; Grenia is often impressed by chef Jessica Wilson's style, rather than just her ingredients. "She does a three-component soup that's incredible—only three ingredients, and there's so much she can do with them!" Grenia aspires to that philosophy in cocktails: "Clean and simple, and with a philosophy of expressing flavor, doing less with more."

The follow-up project next door is dubbed Yours Sincerely—"the other end of the letter that starts with Dear Bushwick"—and will be still more cocktail focused. "We're really trying to push the boundaries there." Twenty-one different cocktails are on draft, everything from glorified highballs to much more original creations. "We're trying to bridge the gap between dive bars—which Bushwick is saturated in—and cocktail bars. Can you get a cocktail at the speed you could get a beer and a shot?"

> " Clean and simple, and with a philosophy of expressing flavor, doing less with more. "
>
> —Darren Grenia, Dear Bushwick

COCKTAIL RECIPES

Smoking Jacket (p. 167)
London's Burning (p. 225)
Windrush (p. 190)
Raisin the Bar (p. 107)

<blockquote>
"We're trying to bridge the gap between dive bars—which Bushwick is saturated in—and cocktail bars. "

—Darren Grenia, *Dear Bushwick*
</blockquote>

4 TAKES ON THE FRENCH 75

The great thing about a French 75: It's equally compelling when made with gin or with Cognac. Lemon, a little sugar, and sparkling wine make this a timeless favorite, whether you opt for the botanical complexity of gin or the brandy version with a bit more weight to it.

ARNAUD'S FRENCH 75
MAISON PREMIERE

"Arnaud's, in New Orleans, is our unofficial sister restaurant—the kind of place where people still wear top hats and smoke cigars inside," says Will Elliott. "Cocktail historian and bartender Chris Hannah, from Arnaud's, researched the French 75 and has a very compelling case that it originated as a Cognac drink. We like to pay it that honor."

1 oz/30 mL Cognac
(Dudognon Reserve recommended)
¼ oz/10 mL lemon juice
¼ oz/10 mL simple syrup
4 oz/120 mL Champagne

In a cocktail shaker with ice, combine the first three ingredients and shake briefly. Pour the Champagne into a flute and strain the cocktail on top. Garnish with a lemon twist, expressed and then balanced on the flute lip.

FRENCH 75 FOR BRUNCH

ACHILLES HEEL

It's not at all orthodox, but "yes, we make our French 75 in a beer mug," says Marie Tribouilloy. "We serve it at brunch; when it's still the afternoon, and you're going to have a cocktail in a beautiful frozen mug, there's a sense of comfort. And sometimes, it's easier just to grab the handle."

1 oz/30 mL gin
½ oz/15 mL honey syrup (1:1)
½ oz/15 mL lemon juice
5 to 6 oz/150 to 180 mL sparkling wine

Combine the first three ingredients in a chilled mug filled with ice. Give it a brief stir, then fill with sparkling wine. Garnish with a lemon twist.

French 75 for Brunch, Achilles Heel

SETTANTACINQUE
TOBIAS ROWER, FRANNY'S

Literally "seventy-five" in Italian, this sparkling drink from Franny's bartender Tobias Rower echoes the original in its lemon and bubbles, but with a base of rye and Luxardo bitter, with red sparkling wine Lambrusco to top.

1 oz/30 mL Luxardo Bitter liqueur
1 oz/30 mL Old Overholt rye
¾ oz/20 mL lemon juice
Lambrusco

In a cocktail shaker with ice, combine the first three ingredients and shake briefly. Strain into a Collins glass over fresh ice and top with Lambrusco. Garnish with a lemon twist.

HAMPTONS 75
TORREY BELL-EDWARDS, WILLOW

"The beach plum is a stone fruit native to New York that adds some intense tartness to the classic French 75," says Torrey Bell-Edwards.

1 oz/30 mL Greenhook beach plum gin
½ oz/15 mL lemon juice
Sparkling wine

In a cocktail shaker with ice, combine the first two ingredients and shake briefly. Strain into a wine glass, top with sparkling wine, and garnish with a lemon twist.

STRONG ISLAND SHANDY

John Bush, Pork Slope

There are classic shandies that cut *down* the proof of beer—and then there are shandies like this "Strong Island," that take beer near a cocktail proof.

2 oz/60 mL Broker's gin
1 oz/30 mL honey syrup (1:1)
1 oz/30 mL lemon juice
3 dashes citrus bitters
Hefeweizen (Southampton White recommended)

Combine all the ingredients except beer in a cocktail shaker with ice. Shake until well chilled and strain into a pint glass filled with ice. Top with Hefeweizen and garnish with a lemon wedge.

SEA SHANDY

David Moo, Quarter Bar

Cel-Ray soda is a New York cult favorite; often sold at Jewish delis, it's refreshing and dry, slightly savory, the kind of thing that tastes like celery only once you know it's there. It's a great match for a pilsner.

3 oz/90 mL Dr. Brown's Cel-Ray soda
½ oz/15 mL lime juice
Pilsner

Rim a pint glass with salt, fill the glass with ice, then add the Cel-Ray and lime juice, topping with pilsner.

Ba'sik

HOW TO TRAVEL

Maks Pazuniak, Jupiter Disco

Beer cocktails aren't all as simple as a shandy; in some, it's just one element of a much more complex cocktail, like this combination of applejack, lemon, and honey topped with a hoppy IPA.

1½ oz/45 mL cinnamon-infused Laird's applejack (recipe p. 264)
¾ oz/20 mL Cinzano sweet vermouth
½ oz/15 mL lemon juice
½ oz/15 mL honey syrup (1:1)
2 dashes Angostura bitters
2 oz/60 mL Lagunitas IPA

Combine all the ingredients except beer in a cocktail shaker with ice. Shake until well chilled and strain into a Collins glass. Top with the IPA.

BLACK VELVET

"This is the perfect brunch cocktail, because it pairs Champagne and stout," says Tonia Guffey of Dram. "It's so easy, and so underrated."

3 oz/90 mL Champagne or sparkling wine
3 oz/90 mL stout

Fill a flute halfway with sparkling wine, then slowly layer stout on top to fill.

THE BEERSKI

David Sheridan, Wheated

This drink builds from sour Gose, which brings vibrant acidity to a whiskey cocktail. "It's the closest I've come to a whiskey sour with the mouthfeel and foam of an egg drink," says David Sheridan, "but without the egg."

2 oz/60 mL tart Gose (Anderson Holy or
Westbrook recommended)
1 oz/30 mL bourbon
½ oz/15 mL simple syrup

Combine all the ingredients in a cocktail shaker with ice, and give a few gentle shakes (not too hard, due to the beer's carbonation). Strain into a Collins glass without ice and top with additional beer, bringing the "head" to the top of the glass.

WINE

FROZEMONADE

Rob Krueger, Extra Fancy

"When you hear *Frozemonade*, you know exactly what this is," says Rob Krueger—a frozen slush of rosé and lemonade, indeed. He notes that a float of any spirit can be added to the top: vodka, tequila, gin . . .

4 oz/120 mL dry rosé wine
¾ oz/20 mL simple syrup
½ oz/15 mL lemon juice

Combine all the ingredients in a blender with 1 cup of ice and blend until smooth. Pour into a glass and garnish with a mint sprig.

AQUA-Y-ESSENCE

Luke Jackson, Do or Dine

Wine meshes beautifully with wine-based Lillet in this stirred drink and, along with grapefruit liqueur pamplemousse, contributes acidity without any fresh fruit juice.

1½ oz/45 mL Dorothy Parker American gin
1 oz/30 mL dry viognier (or a full-bodied
Sauvingon Blanc)
¾ oz/20 mL Lillet Blanc
¼ oz/10 mL Combier pamplemousse
2 dashes grapefruit bitters (or orange bitters,
as a substitute)

Twist a grapefruit peel into a coupe and discard the peel; set the glass aside. Combine all the ingredients in a mixing glass with ice. Stir until well chilled and strain into the coupe.

Redneck Hot Tub, Pork Slope

REDNECK HOT TUB

John Bush, Pork Slope

The name might not be politically correct, but it's hard to fault this dead-simple drink of rosé, Aperol, and soda—a crowd pleaser if ever there were one. (Cheez Doodles are suggested as a "food pairing.")

1 oz/30 mL Aperol
2 oz/60 mL rosé wine
Club soda

Combine first two ingredients in a rocks glass or half-pint glass with ice. Top with soda and garnish with a big orange wedge.

BUBBLES

DEATH IN THE AFTERNOON

Jay Zimmerman, Ba'sik

Most sparkling wine drinks are light and on the fruitier side; but not this Ernest Hemingway favorite, pairing champagne with potent absinthe. Jay Zimmerman's version is civilized, with just a ¼-oz/10-mL pour that won't knock anyone under the table, while the original version has an ounce (30 mL) or more. Up the absinthe at your own risk.

¼ oz/10 mL Pernod absinthe
5 oz/150 mL Prosecco

Pour absinthe into the bottom of a chilled champagne flute or coup and top with Prosecco. Garnish with a lemon twist.

LAMBREWSKI

Torrey Bell-Edwards, Willow

Beer and wine together? It works when the beer is a raspberry ale, and the wine is sparkling red Lambrusco.

2 oz/60 mL Founders Rübaeus raspberry ale (or a raspberry lambic)
½ oz/15 mL limoncello
Lambrusco
1 dash orange bitters

Stir the ale, orange bitters, and limoncello together. Pour into a wine glass, top with Lambrusco, and garnish with a lemon twist.

SEELBACH

Named for the Louisville hotel bar where it was invented, this bourbon sparkler gains flavor and complexity from warm Angostura bitters and anise-flavored Peychaud's; don't skimp on either.

1 oz/30 mL bourbon
½ oz/15 mL Curaçao
7 dashes Peychaud's bitters
7 dashes Angostura bitters
5 oz/150 mL sparkling wine

Combine the first four ingredients in a flute and give it a brief stir. Top with the sparkling wine. Garnish with an orange twist.

CHAMPAGNE COCKTAIL

Dousing a sugar cube in Angostura bitters gives this cocktail a background of warm spice while the sugar cube itself ensures a constant stream of bubbles from the bottom of the flute—striking and elegant.

1 sugar cube
5 to 8 dashes Angostura bitters
5 oz/150 mL Champagne

Add the sugar cube to a flute and dash with Angostura bitters until the cube is saturated. Fill the glass with sparkling wine.

KIR ROYALE

One of the best-known sparkling cocktails; some versions can be cloying and sweet, so it's important to use a light pour (½ oz/15 mL is plenty) and a high-quality cassis (Lejay is a great brand) that echoes the vibrant, sweet-tart flavor of real blackcurrants.

½ oz/15 mL crème de cassis
5 oz/150 mL sparkling wine

Pour cassis into a flute and top with sparkling wine. Garnish with a lemon twist.

ST-GERMAIN SPARKLER

The favorite of many a 21st-century brunch-goer, this simple drink is ideal as a daytime or early evening cocktail, the elderflower liqueur St-Germain a beautiful floral counterpart to the sparkling wine.

½ oz/15 mL St-Germain
5 oz/150 mL sparkling wine

Pour St-Germain into a champagne flute and top with sparkling wine.

NEGRONI SBAGLIATO

Literally an "incorrect" Negroni, the Sbagliato swaps in Prosecco for gin, for a slightly bitter cocktail that's far lighter than its boozier counterpart. The Negroni's 1-1-1 ratios are kept intact here, but the drink is equally tasty, if different in character, served in a flute with 3 oz/90 mL Prosecco.

1 oz/30 mL Campari
1 oz/30 mL sweet vermouth
1 oz/30 mL Prosecco

In a glass with ice, gently stir together all the ingredients. (Alternatively, for a lighter drink, combine the Campari, vermouth, and 3 oz/90 mL Prosecco without ice in a flute.) Garnish with an orange peel.

Rosé at The Narrows

ACHILLES HEEL

Though fairly nondescript from the outside, there's something tremendously atmospheric about the space at Achilles Heel—"The space itself has so much history, and we don't want to forget what it used to be," says bar supervisor Marie Tribouilloy.

That space, all the way west on the river in Greenpoint, opened as a dockworker's bar in 1928. "It used to be open all day and all night; men would unload lumber and, depending on when the ships would arrive, they'd come straight here for food and beer, no matter what time," she says. It closed, reopened as a bar in the 1960s and 1970s, and then closed again before restaurateur Andrew Tarlow, who

" The space itself has so much history, and we don't want to forget what it used to be ... "
—Marie Tribouilloy, Achilles Heel

runs foundational Brooklyn restaurants including Diner, Marlow & Sons, and Reynard, took over the space. Low-ceilinged but flooded with light by daytime, it's an intimate-feeling venue whose history really is palpable. "The space defined what we wanted to do. They kept everything—the floor, the ceiling, the bar. . ."

Tarlow's restaurants are known for constantly changing menus and a sense of informal experimentation, which defines the bar at Achilles as well. "The fact that we're all constantly playing around with things makes it really playful for the customer. We're adaptable, and we're having a lot of fun." The bar team works closely with the kitchen—in a small space, it'd be almost difficult to do otherwise—taking full advantage of each others' ingredients and technique. "The company has been working with the same farmers for so long, so we get the best ingredients. We make our own sodas and shrubs, I use the kitchen's berries to infuse liquor, we're making vermouth . . ."

Their enthusiasm for ingredients becomes apparent when Marie dashes outside to pick a fennel flower garnish for the Main Land cocktail, tequila and sweet vermouth with a beet shrub that's been slowly fermenting for more than a week; or simpler drinks she invents spur-of-the-moment, like the Little Zeddie with mezcal and CioCaro amaro.

Of course, today's menu has few cocktails—few *words*, really—that a Depression-era dockworker would recognize as food or drink. But that doesn't mean their legacy has been forgotten.

COCKTAIL RECIPES

" The fact that we're all constantly playing around with things makes it really playful for the customer. We're adaptable, and we're having a lot of fun. "

—Marie Trilbouilloy, Achilles Heel

Maison Sherry Cobbler,
Maison Premiere

SHERRY

As we've seen in other cocktails throughout this book, bartenders go nuts for sherry. "It adds texture and structure to a cocktail," says Maison Premiere's Will Elliott, "and adds really fun elements you can't get out of other bottles—nuttiness, salinity, oxidization. All those things are fun little things to play around with."

BAMBOO

A classic stirred low-proof drink that highlights medium-bodied oloroso sherry in tandem with dry vermouth.

1½ oz/45 mL oloroso sherry
1½ oz/45 mL Dolin dry vermouth
1 dash orange bitters

Combine all ingredients in a mixing glass with several cracked ice cubes. Stir until well chilled and strain into a coupe. Garnish with a lemon twist.

MAISON SHERRY COBBLER
Maison Premiere

A house favorite, this cocktail is not only a visual showstopper, but a true example of how well sherries can work with many flavors—including fruit, and including each other.

¾ oz/20 mL amontillado sherry
¾ oz/20 mL manzanilla sherry
¾ oz/20 mL oloroso sherry
¾ oz/20 mL Pedro Ximénez sherry
¾ oz/20 mL blueberry or blackberry jam
½ oz/15 mL lemon juice
½ oz/15 mL pineapple juice
¼ oz/10 mL demerara syrup (1:1)
1 tsp/5 mL allspice dram

Combine all the ingredients in a cocktail shaker with ice. Shake until well chilled and strain into a poco grande glass (similar to a Hurricane glass) or similar, filled with crushed ice. Garnish with two halved blackberries, a thin half-moon slice of orange, and a bouquet of mint, along with a straw.

CLOVER CLUB

THE INGREDIENTS

Housemade syrups, tinctures, infusions, and even bitters are essential to Brooklyn bars. These ingredients can sound complicated—lapsang souchong syrup? Lime-ginger cordial? But from a culinary perspective, making them tends to be dead simple. If you can heat up sugar and water, you can make any of the syrups below; if you have a bottle and a funnel and don't mind waiting 24 hours, you can make any of the infused spirits. Of course, it takes a good deal of time and patience for bartenders to develop these recipes, such that they perform just right in a cocktail—but the work to make them? That's easy.

Some of these (cinnamon syrup, vanilla syrup) require just minutes of work, and ingredients you may already have in your pantry; others are a bit more involved, and a few, for the true cocktail geeks only. (Fermenting your own beet shrub: Awesome when you get it right, but a pretty intense process.)

Having to create a ginger syrup before you even start shaking a cocktail may seem just too complicated, and of course if you're looking for a quick drink, it's not that practical. But once you've made the ginger syrup, it'll keep for weeks—and not only can you make that favorite cocktail night after night, but you can play around with it in other cocktails, too. And infused spirits? They'll last virtually forever. (Or make an unbeatable holiday or party gift.)

So devote five minutes to making a simple thyme-infused gin, or chamomile honey, and see where it takes you. Once you've got your housemade ingredients sitting around, you'll be itching to use them—and how impressed will your friends be that you infused your own gin?

CHAPTER 10

SPIRITS

CINNAMON-INFUSED APPLEJACK

How to Travel, Jupiter Disco

1 750-mL bottle Laird's Bottled in
  Bond applejack
8 cinnamon sticks

Pour the applejack into a sealable containe
and add cinnemon sticks. Let infuse for 24
hours, strain, and return the infused applejack
to the bottle.

ONCE YOU'VE MADE IT ...

CINNAMON-APPLE OLD
FASHIONED: A perfectly autumnal
stirred drink with a strong aroma of apples
and cinnamon (2 oz/60 mL cinnamon
applejack, ½ oz/15 mL honey syrup, 1 dash
of orange bitters and 1 dash of Angostura
bitters, stirred, strained into rocks glass with
ice, garnished with a lemon peel)

CINNAMON-APPLE TODDY:
Bringing the rich apple-cinnamon flavor to a
comforting hot toddy (2 oz/60 mL cinnamon
applejack, ½ oz/15 mL demerara syrup, 1
dash of Angostura bitters, 3 oz/90 mL boiling
water, stir, garnish with a squeezed lemon
wedge, stud three cloves in lemon wedge
and leave in drink)

CINNAMON-APPLE CIDER:
A dead-simple method for a refreshing fall
drink (1½ oz/45 mL cinnamon applejack,
6 oz/180 mL hard cider, stirred together in
a pint glass over ice)

CUCUMBER & PINK PEPPERCORN-INFUSED VODKA

Stone of Jordan, Roberta's

1 750-mL bottle vodka
1 cucumber, peeled
½ cup/55 g whole pink peppercorns

Slice the cucumber. Grind ½ cup of whole
pink peppercorn in a spice grinder (or
blender) until fine. Make a cheesecloth pouch
with the sliced cucumber and ground
peppercorns inside. Pour the vodka into a
sealable container. Soak cucumber–pink
peppercorn cheesecloth in the vodka for 3
days. Remove the cheesecloth and strain the
infused vodka back into the bottle.

LEMONGRASS-INFUSED VODKA

Porch Swing Collins, Butter & Scotch

1 750-mL bottle Reyka vodka
3 stalks lemongrass

Chop the lemongrass into small pieces.
Add to a blender with the vodka and blend
until the lemongrass is well blended. Strain

San Francisco Handshake, Hotel Delmano

through a chinois or fine sieve, discard the lemongrass, and strain the vodka back into bottle.

ONCE YOU'VE MADE IT …

LEMONGRASS '75: It's important not to add too many competing flavors to something subtle like lemongrass, which is why lemon and sparkling wine are ideal (1½ oz/45 mL lemongrass-infused vodka, ½ oz/15 mL simple syrup, ½ oz/15 mL lemon juice, shaken together, strained into a flute and topped with 2½ oz/75 mL sparkling wine)

LEMONGRASS GIMLET:
Lemongrass comes through even more clearly in this simple gimlet (2 oz/60 mL lemongrass-infused vodka, 1 oz/30 mL lime juice, ¾ oz/20 mL simple syrup, shaken, strained into a coupe)

THYME-INFUSED GIN
San Francisco Handshake, Hotel Delmano

1 750-mL bottle gin
Large bunch of fresh thyme

Pour the gin into a sealable container and add thyme. Let infuse for 24 hours, strain, and return the infused gin to the bottle.

ONCE YOU'VE MADE IT …

THYME G&T: A simple showcase for the infused gin's herbal flavors (2 oz/60 mL thyme gin, 4 oz/120 mL Fever Tree tonic in a Collins glass with ice, brief stir, garnish with a thyme sprig and lime wedge)

THYME COLLINS: Integrating the thyme gin into a bright, lemony tall drink (1½ oz/45 mL thyme gin, ½ oz/15 mL lemon juice, ½ oz/15 mL simple syrup, shaken; strain into a Collins glass filled with ice, top with 3 oz/90 mL soda, garnish with a lemon wheel and thyme sprig)

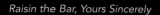
Raisin the Bar, Yours Sincerely

RAISIN RYE

Raisin the Bar, Yours Sincerely

1 750-mL bottle Rittenhouse rye
¾ cup raisins

Add raisins to the rye bottle and replace the cap. Let infuse for 24 hours, strain out the raisins (and save for garnishing), and return the infused rye to the bottle.

ONCE YOU'VE MADE IT . . .

RAISIN OLD FASHIONED: Let the spirit shine in a simple drink made rich by the body and depth of raisin-steeped rye (2 oz/60 mL raisin rye, ½ oz/15 mL demerara syrup, 1 dash of Angostura bitters, stir, strain into rocks glass with ice, garnish with an orange peel and rye-soaked raisins)

RAISIN FLIP: Rich and satisfying almost in the way of eggnog, or rum-raisin ice cream (2 oz/60 mL raisin rye, 1 oz/30 mL simple syrup, 1 dash Angostura bitters, 1 whole egg; dry shake all in a cocktail shaker without ice, then add ice and wet shake; strain into rocks glass without ice, garnish with fresh-grated nutmeg and/or rye-soaked raisins)

COCONUT RUM

Belafonte, Roberta's

1 750-ml bottle white rum
2 cups unsweetened desiccated coconut

Pour the rum into a sealable container. Add the desiccated coconut. Soak for 3 days. Strain out the coconut and return the infused rum to the bottle.

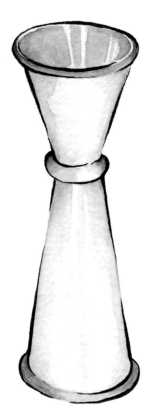

GENMAICHA GREEN TEA RUM

Forbidden Planet, Donna

1 1-L bottle Plantation 3 Stars rum
1 oz/30 mL Genmaicha green tea

Add the green tea to the rum bottle and cover. Steep for 20 minutes, then strain through a fine strainer or a chinois. Return the infused rum to the bottle.

Leyenda

JALAPEÑO-INFUSED TEQUILA

There are many different methods for infusing jalapeño into tequila; this one contributes quite a bit of heat, with some of the jalapeño's vegetal green-pepper flavor but not too much. Depending on the jalapeños you get, the time it takes to impart the heat can vary wildly. Start tasting as soon as half an hour, but be prepared to let it sit quite a bit longer.

1 750-mL bottle blanco tequila
2 jalapeño peppers

Slice 1 jalapeño pepper to expose seeds, and add the pepper (including seeds) to the bottle of tequila. Take just the seeds and membranes of the other jalapeño and add that too. Let sit for 30 minutes, and taste to determine level of heat; continue to steep until desired spiciness is reached.

CHIPOTLE-INFUSED MEZCAL
Devil's Garden, Hotel Delmano

1 750-mL bottle mezcal
2 dried, crushed chipotle peppers

Add the chipotle to the mezcal bottle and replace the cap. Let infuse for 24 hours, strain, and return the infused mezcal to the bottle.

ONCE YOU'VE MADE IT ...

CHIPOTLE MANHATTAN:
A strong dose of sweet vermouth and rich, bittersweet Cynar result in an amazing, smoky-spicy sipper (2 oz/60 mL chipotle mezcal, 1 oz/30 mL Carpano Antica Formula sweet vermouth, ¼ oz/10 mL Cynar, ¼ oz/ 10 mL agave syrup, 1 dash of Angostura bitters, stir, strain into coupe, garnish with a grapefruit twist)

CHIPOTLE PALOMA:
Tall and refreshing, but without losing any of the intensity of your smoky chipotle-infused spirit (1½ oz/45 mL chipotle mezcal, 1½ oz/45 mL ruby red grapefruit juice, ½ oz/15 mL agave syrup, 1 dash grapefruit bitters, shake; strain into a Collins glass filled with ice, top with 1 oz/30 mL soda)

YERBA MATE-INFUSED PISCO
Buena Onda, Leyenda

1 750-mL bottle pisco
2 tablespoons loose mate

Add the mate to the pisco bottle and replace the cap. Let infuse for 15 minutes, fine-strain, and return the infused pisco to the bottle.

JALAPEÑO TINCTURE
La Guernica, The Drink

5 jalapeño peppers, sliced, seeds removed
High-proof vodka

In a small jar or container, cover peppers with vodka. Cover, let sit for 3 hours, and strain.

FRUIT INFUSIONS

MARASCHINO CHERRY VODKA
East Ender, Roberta's

1 750-ml bottle vodka
10 oz/300 g jar maraschino cherries

Pour vodka into blender and add the whole jar of cherries. Blend on high for 2 to 3 minutes. Strain into container and decant back into bottle.

ONCE YOU'VE MADE IT...

CHERRY MOJITO: This cherry vodka/"liqueur" is nothing but fun, a total party drink, and it works perfectly in a simple mojito (Cut half a lime into three wedges; muddle in the bottom of a cocktail shaker, add 5 to 8 mint leaves, 2 oz/60 mL cherry vodka, ¾ oz/20 mL simple syrup, about 4 ice cubes, shake vigorously, pour cocktail (ice and all) into Collins glass, add 2 oz/60 mL club soda, stir, garnish with a straw and mint sprig)

CHERRY COKE: What's a better use for anything cherry-flavored than a boozy cherry Coke? (2 oz/60 mL cherry vodka and 4 oz/120 mL Coca-Cola, served over ice in a Collins glass, garnished with a lemon wedge)

CANTALOUPE LIQUEUR

Cantaloupe Shandy, Roberta's

1 750-ml bottle vodka
1 medium-size cantaloupe

Slice the cantaloupe flesh into cubes. Pour the vodka into a sealable container and add the cantaloupe. Let soak for 3 days. Muddle the cantaloupe chunks in the vodka and double strain. Return infused vodka to the bottle.

ONCE YOU'VE MADE IT ...

CANTALOUPE & MINT: A simple brunchtime cocktail that pairs the cantaloupe with a bright burst of mint (2 oz/60 mL cantaloupe liqueur, ¾ oz/20 mL lemon juice, ½ oz/15 mL simple syrup, 10 mint leaves, shake together and double-strain into a Collins glass with ice, top with soda)

CANTALOUPE & BASIL: A slightly more unusual herbal-fruit pairing that works beautifully in a shaken drink, served up (2 oz/60 mL cantaloupe liqueur, ¾ oz/20 mL lime juice, ½ oz/15 mL simple syrup, 8 basil leaves, shake together with ice, double-strain into a coupe, garnish with a basil leaf)

NOTE: The "oz" measurements for granulated sugar in this section are fluid ounces. The assumption is that, given the tools of the trade, a bartender would measure by volume instead of weight.

SYRUPS AND SUCH

The sugar in cocktail syrups gives them an extremely long shelf life; kept refrigerated, they'll keep for at least a few weeks.

CINNAMON SYRUP

1 cup/240 mL white sugar
1 cinnamon stick
1 cup/240 mL water

Combine the sugar and water over low heat in a saucepan. Stir gently to dissolve the sugar. Add the cinnamon stick and continue stirring until all of the sugar has dissolved. Turn off the heat, cover, and let stand for 2 to 3 hours. Remove the cinnamon sticks and strain the liquid into a container that can be closed and refrigerated.

ONCE YOU'VE MADE IT ...

CINNAMON OLD FASHIONED: The whiskey-bitters-citrus triad of an Old Fashioned adapts perfectly to a bit of cinnamon (2 oz/60 mL bourbon, ½ oz/15 mL cinnamon syrup, 1 dash of orange bitters and 1 dash of Angostura bitters, stir, strain into rocks glass with ice, garnish with an orange and a lemon peel)

CINNAMON & TEQUILA: Reposado (slightly aged) tequila works well with warm spices, and cinnamon fits the bill perfectly (2 oz/60 mL reposado tequila, ½ oz/15 mL sweet vermouth, ½ oz/15 mL cinnamon syrup and 2 dashes of Angostura bitters, stir, strain into rocks glass with ice, garnish with a lime peel)

Back of the Bar, Roberta's

VANILLA SYRUP

1 cup/240 mL white sugar
1 whole vanilla bean
1 cup/240 mL water

Slice the vanilla bean along its length to expose the seeds inside. Combine the sugar and water over low heat in a saucepan. Stir gently to dissolve the sugar. Add the vanilla bean and continue stirring until all of the sugar has dissolved. Turn off the heat, cover, and let stand for 2 to 3 hours. Remove the vanilla bean and strain the liquid into a container that can be closed and refrigerated.

ONCE YOU'VE MADE IT ...

VANILLA SOUR: Take the vanilla-caramel flavors of bourbon and draw them out in this classic sour with egg white to add a silky texture (½ oz/45 mL bourbon, ¾ oz/20 mL lemon juice, ¾ oz/20 mL vanilla syrup, 1 egg white; dry shake all in a cocktail shaker without ice, add ice, wet shake, strain into a chilled coupe)

VANILLA TODDY: Real vanilla bean deserves a high-quality spirit like Cognac in this sophisticated hot toddy (2 oz/60 mL Cognac, ½ oz/15 mL vanilla syrup, 3 oz/90 mL boiling water, stir together in a mug, garnish with a squeezed lemon wedge and coin-shaped orange peel studded with three cloves)

Hotel Delmano

VANILLA-DEMERARA SYRUP

Enoch's Folly, Esme

Follow procedure for vanilla syrup, using demerara sugar.

MOLASSES SIMPLE SYRUP

½ cup/120 mL molasses (do not use blackstrap molasses)
½ cup/120 mL water

Combine water and molasses in a saucepan. Heat and stir until the molasses has dissolved; do not boil. Store in a container that can be closed and refrigerated.

LIME SYRUP

Rum, Sodomy, and the Lash, Tooker Alley

1 cup/240 mL simple syrup
4 limes

Zest the limes into the simple syrup. Cover and refrigerate for 24 hours. Strain.

GINGER SYRUP

1 whole hand of fresh ginger
White sugar

Juice the ginger using a juicer, or in a food processor or blender (blend with a little water until liquid, then strain). Measure ginger juice, and combine 1 part fresh ginger juice with the allotted amount of sugar (see below). Stir until all the sugar has dissolved. Will keep refrigerated up to 1 month.

For The Ninety-Nine Roses (Hotel Delmano), New Rider (Rucola), Extra-Ginger Dark & Stormy, Ginger Caipirinha, Happy/Sad Girl (No. 7), Arch Leveler (Bearded Lady), Cool Leatherette (Sisters): 1 part ginger juice to 1 part sugar

For Watership Down (Donna), Infernal Affairs (Donna), Smoking Jacket (Dear Bushwick): 1 part ginger juice to 2 parts sugar

For Poppa's Pride (Ba'sik): 3 parts ginger juice to 1 part sugar

ONCE YOU'VE MADE IT ...
(1:1 ginger to sugar)

GINGER & TEQUILA: Ginger's bite and tequila's bite mesh well in this tall refresher (2 oz/60 mL blanco tequila, 1 oz/30 mL lime juice, ¾ oz/20 mL ginger syrup, shaken; strain into a Collins glass filled with ice, top with 2 oz/60 mL soda, garnish with a lime wheel)

GINGER-RYE SOUR: Rye's spice and ginger are a smart match in a sour (2 oz/60 mL rye, 1 oz/30 mL lemon juice, ¾ oz/20 mL ginger syrup, shaken; strain into a rocks glass filled with ice, garnish with brandied cherries)

ANCHO SIMPLE SYRUP

Oaxaca Floca Flame, Mayfield

1 cup/240 mL white sugar
1 cup/240 mL water
2 ancho chiles, torn into rough pieces

Combine the sugar and water over low heat in a saucepan. Stir gently to dissolve the sugar. Add the chiles. Turn off the heat, cover, and let stand for 2 to 3 hours. Remove chiles and strain liquid into a container that can be closed and refrigerated.

PINEAPPLE SYRUP

Wire + String, Jupiter Disco

½ small fresh pineapple
White sugar

Juice the pineapple using a juicer or in a food processor (blend until liquid, then strain). Measure pineapple juice, and combine 1 part pineapple juice with 1 part sugar. Stir until the sugar dissolves.

RASPBERRY SYRUP

Clover Club, Clover Club

½ cup/75 g raspberries
1 cup/240 mL sugar
½ cup/120 mL water

Mash up the raspberries in a small pot. Add the sugar and water. Over very low heat—do not boil—stir to dissolve the sugar. Once the sugar is mostly dissolved, remove from the heat and let the mixture sit for 30 minutes. Stir to dissolve any remaining sugar, then strain out the solids. Refrigerate.

ONCE YOU'VE MADE IT ...

RASPBERRY-RUM SOUR:
A lively summer sour, bringing out the raspberry's acidity with lemon, with a refreshing hit of mint (2 oz/60 mL white rum, 1 oz/30 mL lemon juice, ½ oz/15 mL raspberry syrup, 1 dash orange bitters, 8 mint leaves; shake, double-strain into a rocks glass with fresh ice and a splash of club soda, garnish with a lemon wheel and a raspberry)

RASPBERRY VODKA SODA:
The world's simplest highball lets this raspberry syrup shine, with a big squeeze of lemon to bump up the acid (2 oz/60 mL vodka, ½ oz/15 mL raspberry syrup in a Collins glass with ice, fill with about 4 oz/120 mL club soda, garnish with a big lemon wedge squeezed into the drink)

BLUEBERRY SYRUP

Bourbon Blueberry Crumble,
Kings County Distillery

2 pints/2 L blueberries
1 cup/240 mL water
1 cup/240 mL sugar

Blend the blueberries and water in a blender on high for 2 minutes and strain. Combine the juice and sugar in a small pot and cook over low heat, stirring often, just until the sugar dissolves. Remove from the heat and let cool.

ONCE YOU'VE MADE IT ...

BLUEBERRY SOUR: An easy-drinking cocktail ideal for a summer brunch or garden party (1½ oz/45 mL gin, 1½ oz/45 mL blueberry syrup, 1 oz/30 mL lemon juice; shake, strain into a rocks glass with crushed ice, garnish with a few blueberries)

BLUEBERRIES & BOURBON:
Blueberry can pair well with dark spirits, too, as in this shaken mint-lemon-bourbon drink (1½ oz/45 mL bourbon, 1 oz/30 mL blueberry syrup, ½ oz/15 mL lemon juice, 10 mint leaves; shake, double-strain into a rocks glass with fresh ice, garnish with 3 mint sprigs and a few blueberries)

RED BELL PEPPER SYRUP

Drinking at the Gym, Huckleberry Bar

2 to 3 red bell peppers
Powdered chipotle pepper
Smoked Spanish paprika
White sugar

Juice the bell peppers, and measure resulting juice. For every cup yielded, add 1/4 teaspoon chipotle pepper and 1/4 tablespoon smoked Spanish paprika. Bring that mixture to a boil, and add an equal amount of sugar to the juice, stirring until the sugar is dissolved. Once the sugar is dissolved, remove from the heat, let cool, then strain into a sealable container and refrigerate.

CUCUMBER SYRUP

Faith and Fortitude, Huckleberry Bar

1 cucumber, peeled and sliced
½ cup/120 mL water
Simple syrup

In a blender, thoroughly purée the cucumber and water until fully liquified. Strain to get cucumber juice and measure. Add an equal amount of simple syrup to cucumber juice. Stir to combine, seal, and refrigerate.

ONCE YOU'VE MADE IT ...

CUCUMBER-ELDERFLOWER COLLINS: Lemon lifts the already-refreshing cucumber and a small measure of St-Germain adds an intriguing floral element (1½ oz/45 mL vodka, 1 oz/30 mL cucumber syrup, ¾ oz/20 mL lemon juice, and ¼ oz/10 mL St-Germain; shake, strain into a Collins glass over ice, top with 2 oz/60 mL soda, garnish with a basil leaf)

CUCUMBER 75: A French 75 made lighter and brighter with cucumber (¾ oz/20 mL gin, ¾ oz/20 mL cucumber syrup, ½ oz/15 mL lemon juice, shake, strain into a flute, top with 4 oz/120 mL sparkling wine, garnish with a cucumber wheel)

RHUBARB SYRUP

Alice's Mallet, Quarter Bar

1½ lbs/750 g fresh rhubarb
¼ cup/60 g sugar
½ oz/15 mL lemon juice

Cut the rhubarb into 1-inch/25-mm chunks, and place in a pot with the sugar. Add about ½ cup/120 mL water (just enough to keep rhubarb from burning). Cover and bring up to a simmer. Cook for about 10 minutes, until the rhubarb has become soft and rendered its liquids. Press in batches through a fine-mesh strainer, reserving liquid. Add the lemon juice as a color preservative and refrigerate.

ROSEMARY SYRUP

Rosarita, Quarter Bar

1¾ cup/420 mL sugar
1¾ cup/420 mL water
3 to 4 oz/90 to 120 g fresh rosemary

Combine the sugar and water over low heat in a saucepan until just boiling, stirring to dissolve the sugar, then reduce heat. Add the rosemary, cover, and remove from heat. Let stand for 60 minutes. Remove the rosemary and strain the liquid into a container that can be closed and refrigerated.

ONCE YOU'VE MADE IT ...

ROSEMARY COLLINS: Rosemary is a pleasantly familiar herbal addition to a classic lemon-gin-soda Collins (2 oz/60 mL gin, ½ oz/15 mL lemon juice, ½ oz/15 mL rosemary syrup, shake, strain into a Collins glass with ice, fill with about 2 oz/60 mL club soda, garnish with a rosemary sprig)

ROSEMARY-APPLE SOUR: Apples and rosemary pair well, so applejack is a perfect base for a rosemary sour (2 oz/60 mL Laird's Bottled in Bond applejack, ¾ oz/20 mL lemon juice, ¾ oz/20 mL rosemary syrup; shake, strain into a rocks glass with fresh ice, garnish with a rosemary sprig)

MINT SYRUP

La Tempesta, Franny's

1¾ cup/420 mL sugar
1¾ cup/420 mL water
Small bunch of mint

Combine the sugar and water over low heat in a saucepan until just boiling, stirring to dissolve the sugar, then reduce heat. Add mint, cover, and remove from heat. Let stand for 60 minutes. Remove the mint and strain the liquid into a container that can be closed and refrigerated.

LAPSANG SYRUP
Jupiter Disco

½ oz/60 mL Lapsang Souchong tea
  (about 4 teabags)
1 cup/240 mL demerara sugar
1 cup/240 mL hot water

Steep the tea in the hot water (approx. 180 to 190 degrees), then strain. Add the demerara sugar to tea and stir until dissolved.

ONCE YOU'VE MADE IT …

LAPSANG OLD FASHIONED:
This intensely smoky tea, which seems to taste of smoked wood and barbecue, works perfectly with bourbon (2 oz/60 mL bourbon, ½ oz/15 mL lapsang syrup, 2 dashes of Angostura bitters, stir, strain into rocks glass with ice, garnish with an orange peel)

LAPSANG ICED TEA: Lapsang
souchong is a tea, after all, so an iced tea format is incredible: blended Scotch to pick up the smokiness (though not add to it too much), lemon, the sweetness from the syrup, and club soda to lighten it up (2 oz/60 mL blended Scotch whiskey, such as Famous Grouse, ¾ oz/20 mL lemon juice, ¾ oz/20 mL lapsang syrup, shake, strain into a Collins glass with fresh ice, top with 2 oz/60 mL soda, garnish with a lemon wheel)

LAPSANG SYRUP
The Drink

1 Lapsang souchong teabag
6 oz/180 mL sugar
6 oz/180 mL hot water

Steep the tea in the hot water for 5 to 7 minutes, remove the teabag, and let cool. Add the sugar to the tea and stir until dissolved.

HIBISCUS SYRUP
La Guernica, The Drink

1 hibiscus teabag
6 oz/180 mL sugar
6 oz/180 mL hot water

Steep tea in hot water for 5 to 7 minutes, remove the teabag, and let cool. Add the sugar to the tea and stir until dissolved.

CHAMOMILE HONEY
Box of Rain, Achilles Heel and O.V. C., Ba'sik

1 Tbsp loose chamomile tea
1 cup/240 mL honey
1 cup/240 mL hot water

Steep the tea in the hot water, let cool, then strain. Add 1 equal part honey to the tea and stir until dissolved. For O.V.C (Ba'sik): Add 3 parts honey to the tea and stir until dissolved.

The Arnaud Palmer, Loosey Rouge

ONCE YOU'VE MADE IT ...

CHAMOMILE SCOTCH SOUR:
Floral chamomile plays well with Scotch in this light sour (2 oz/60 mL blended Scotch, ¾ oz/20 mL lemon juice, ¾ oz/20 mL chamomile honey; shake, strain into a coupe, garnish with a lime wheel)

CHAMOMILE MARGARITA:
Tequila's grassy character emerges with the pairing of chamomile (2 oz/60 mL blanco tequila, ¾ oz/20 mL lemon juice, ¾ oz/20 mL chamomile honey; shake, strain into a rocks glass with fresh ice, garnish with a lemon wheel)

Extra Fancy

CHAMOMILE SYRUP

*The Close Haul and The Old Gunwale,
The Drink*

1 chamomile teabag
6 oz/180 mL sugar
6 oz/180 mL hot water

Steep the tea in the hot water for 5 to 7
minutes, remove the teabag, and let cool.
Add the sugar to the tea and stir until
dissolved.

GREEN TEA SYRUP

Grace O'Malley, The Drink

1 green tea bag
5 oz/150 mL sugar
5 oz/150 mL hot water

Steep the tea in the hot water for 5 the 7
minutes, remove the teabag, and let cool.
Add the sugar to the tea and stir until
dissolved.

CILANTRO SYRUP

Margarita de Pepino, Gran Electrica

½ pint whole cilantro leaves
1 cup/240 mL white sugar
1 cup/240 mL water

Heat the water to boiling and then mix all the
ingredients together, stirring to dissolve the
sugar. Once the sugar is fully dissolved, cool
and refrigerate the syrup. After 48 hours,
strain out the cilantro.

LIME-GINGER CORDIAL

L.I.B. Gimlet, Long Island Bar

Toby Cecchini's cordial starts with an "oleo-saccharum," a technique once used for punch, where sugar essentially draws the oils out of citrus peels.

6 ripe limes, heavy and with shiny skins
1 cup plus 1 Tbs/255 mL white sugar
8 oz/240 g fresh ginger, cleaned and peeled and chopped into ¼ to ½-inch/5- to 10-mm discs

Clean the limes and, with a sharp vegetable peeler, peel them, taking as little of the underlying white pith as possible. In a capacious, nonreactive, coverable container, combine the peels well with the sugar. Cover and leave for 24 hours at room temperature to make an oleosaccharum. Cover and refrigerate the lime fruit.

The following day, juice the limes. In a blender, combine the ginger and lime juice and blend until the ginger has been coarsely chopped. Add this slurry to the oleosaccharum and mix well with a wooden spoon. Set this aside for at least another 24 to 48 hours, stirring every 12 hours or so. Adjust for sweetness; it should be thick and viscous, slightly sweeter than you'd like it pure, as you'll add fresh lime juice in the Gimlet. Strain into a clean, cappable bottle and refrigerate.

L.I.B. Gimlet, Long Island Bar

SHRUBS

A shrub is a syrup of fruit, sugar, and vinegar—concentrated flavors of fresh, sweet, and tart. They make excellent cocktail ingredients, thanks to these multifaceted flavors. Below are two shrub recipes: one quite simple, the other quite ambitious.

STRAWBERRY SHRUB

The Belafonte, Roberta's

1 pint fresh strawberries
1 cup/240 mL white sugar
6 oz/180 mL Champagne vinegar
½ cup/120 mL water

Combine all the ingredients in a blender. Blend on high for 2 to 3 minutes. Pour into a saucepan and cook on medium heat for 45 minutes, stirring occasionally. Let the shrub cool and pour into a sealable container. Decant into a bottle.

ONCE YOU'VE MADE IT...

SHRUB & RUM: The fruity-sour shrub is incredible with funky Jamaican rum and ginger beer to add a little spice and lift (2 oz/60 mL Jamaican rum such as Appleton Reserve, 1 oz/30 mL strawberry shrub; stir in a Collins glass over ice, add 4 oz/120 mL of ginger beer to fill, garnish with a lime wedge)

SHRUB & VODKA: If you want to appreciate a shrub in its own right, pairing it with vodka plus lemon to maintain the acidity is an easy way (2 oz/60 mL vodka, 1 oz/30 mL lemon juice, ¾ oz/20 mL strawberry shrub, 1 dash of orange bitters; shake, strain over fresh ice, garnish with a strawberry)

BEET SHRUB

Main Land, Achilles Heel

Combining fruit, vinegar, and sugar is one way to get acidity in a shrub; for a next-level effervescent, pungent shrub, let the shrub ferment.

1 cup/240 mL beet juice
¼ cup/60 mL Bragg's Organic Apple
  Cider Vinegar

Mix the ingredients together in a jar. Cover tightly with cheesecloth and let stand at room temperature for approximately 1 week. When mold begins to form on top, scrape it off, cover the jar, and refrigerate. It may be 2 or more weeks before the beet shrub becomes effervescent and reaches the right acidity.

AND MORE

AGUA DE JAMAICA

King's Town Punch, Quarter Bar

This hibiscus iced tea is popular in the Caribbean, Latin America, and beyond; it's worth making on its own, whether or not you use it in Quarter Bar's cocktail.

2 oz/60 g jamaica flowers (dried hibiscus)
  by weight, approx. ⅔ rocks glass
6 cups/1.5 L water
¾ cup/180 mL sugar
¼-inch/5-mm disk fresh ginger, grated
1 Tbsp/15 mL lime juice

Boil the water with the ginger. Remove from the heat. Add the flowers and sugar and stir. Steep for 60 minutes. Strain, add the lime juice, and cool.

CHILI-STOUT REDUCTION

Windrush and Smoking Jacket, Dear Bushwick

1 12-oz/360-mL can Lion Stout
  (or another rich, high-ABV stout)
3 cups/720 mL Sugar in the Raw
1 tsp/5 g chili powder

Combine the sugar and stout over low heat in a saucepan, stirring to dissolve the sugar, then reduce heat. Add the chili powder, simmer for 5 minutes, and let cool.

Redneck Hot Tub, left, and Capone's Cocktail, right, Pork Slope

ACKNOWLEDGMENTS

First and foremost, this book is the work of Brooklyn's many talented bartenders, bar owners, and managers, who contributed their recipes, advice, and expertise. Their inventive cocktails, informed opinions, and beautiful establishments animate this text, and hopefully, the spirits of these remarkable bars shine through.

Thanks to my agent Vicky Bijur and editor Dinah Dunn, as well as all the good folks at Black Dog & Leventhal. Thanks to friends throughout the industry who lent their taste-testing opinions; I hope the task wasn't too arduous.

And thanks above all to my very favorite bartender, the professional consultant and recipe tester for this book—my in-house mixologist, industry advisor, and fiancé, John McCarthy. You taught me everything I know about cocktails—I'm so glad I get to spend the rest of my life learning (and drinking) more with you. Cheers.

Grand Army

INDEX

NOTE: *Italic* page numbers indicate photographs.

The Narrows

Maison Premiere

The Richardson

Hotel Delmano

Bottles and decor, Dear Bushwick

Extra Fancy

Grand Army

NOTES